Voices of this

Voices of this Calling

Experiences of the First Generation
of Women Priests

Edited by

Christina Rees

CANTERBURY
PRESS
Norwich

© The Editors and Contributors 2002

First published in 2002 by the Canterbury Press Norwich
(a publishing imprint of Hymns Ancient & Modern Limited,
a registered charity)
St Mary's Works, St Mary's Plain,
Norwich, Norfolk, NR3 3BH

www.scm-canterburypress.co.uk

British Library Cataloguing in Publication data

A catalogue record for this book is available
from the British Library

ISBN 1-85311-412-X

Typeset by Regent Typesetting, London
Printed and bound by
Biddles Ltd, www.biddles.co.uk

This book is dedicated to all women called by God to priesthood in the Church of England.

Contents

Acknowledgements

Many people have helped to make this book happen. I am particularly grateful to Dr Anna Hardman, Senior Editor at SCM-Canterbury Press, for asking me to edit this book and for providing ongoing assistance and encouragement.

I am indebted to my husband, Chris, for all his technological expertise and for his loving, good-natured and generous support. My thanks also to my daughters, Angela and Alexandra, who gave me much practical assistance and who always help me to keep a broader perspective on life!

Most of all, I would like to thank all the women and men who contributed so enthusiastically to this volume. You have taken the time and care to record your voices for posterity, and many of you have also taken the risk to trust the rest of us with your intimate thoughts and experiences. This is your book – thank you.

Christina Rees
July 2002

Part One

Setting the Scene

Setting the Scene

CHRISTINA REES

In the Assembly Hall in Church House, Westminster on Wednesday, 11 November 1992, there is a tense hush. Synod members have returned to their seats after voting by walking through different doors. The Archbishop of Canterbury, Dr George Carey, is in the Chair. He clears his throat and asks the Synod to listen to the results of the voting in silence. It is nearly 5:00pm. He reads: 'House of Bishops, Ayes 39, Noes 13; House of Clergy, Ayes 176, Noes 74; House of Laity, Ayes 169, Noes 82. There being the required number of votes in each House, I declare the motion carried.'

Up in the press gallery there is a muffled squeak: a female journalist throws her arms around a Synod member who is standing by to be interviewed by the BBC. A frisson of excitement runs through the vast room. Unknown to Synod members, the news has reached the crowds gathered outside in Dean's Yard, and there people cheer and burst into tears and singing. Inside, the Archbishop of York calmly takes the Chair, and business continues, with voting on various Amending Canons and on the Financial Provisions contained in the Measure. It has happened: history has been made. Women will be priests in the Church of England.

Ten years after that decisive vote in General Synod is a good time to reflect on the past decade, and to hear from some of the women who went on to become priests. Some of the first women priests were members of that Synod and cast their votes that day. Others were in Dean's Yard surrounded by the group of jubilant supporters. Some listened to the result on radio, or watched it later on the television news. All had been waiting, some for many years, and they knew their lives would be changed, one way or the other, by the outcome of the vote.

Overall, not just those in the Church, but many others across the country celebrated. The Church was alive after all! It could follow the leading of the Holy Spirit. It was relevant. It could change. It valued women.

It is perhaps this last point that took so many, inside and outside the Church, believers and agnostics, by surprise. Women who had not been into a church since childhood, broke down and wept. Men, upon hearing the news, choked up, overcome. Inevitably traditionalists in the Church felt dismay, but many others felt extreme joy, a sense of new possibilities, of hope, of something deep and profound that had been realigned. Women, especially, tell of a new sense of feeling accepted, of feeling affirmed – a sense of worth. The Church *could* bring – and be – good news.

Of course, there were those who did not celebrate when the vote was passed. For them, the Church they had known, loved and served ceased to exist. For them, on 11 November 1992 the walls caved in and a cold wind began to rage. One of the speakers in the debate used the language of catastrophe in his speech against the Measure. The Revd Peter Geldard described the move to ordain women to the priesthood as the Church being asked to 'push down one of the walls that holds the very house together'. Later, he used the image of a woodman taking an axe to the base of the tree: 'before you decide to take your axe or even make a change, consider what it is you do, for in your enthusiasm you may change and destroy more than any of us ever understands' (Report of Proceedings, November 1992 23/3, pp. 726–27).

In a strange way, many of those opposed to the measure intuited that ordaining women as priests would cause profound changes in the Church, much greater than the presence of women in the sanctuary. In a way, Peter Geldard was right: the walls were coming down; the tree was in danger, but he could not see how inhospitable the house had become for so many, nor how weakened was the tree.

After the vote, Peter Geldard was one of those who left the Church of England: at least he knew his conscience on the matter, and did not wait for years, as some have done, to take the money and go. Since then, the Church has paid out over £20 million to men under the Financial Provisions in the Measure. Of the 400 male clergy who have left the Church, over 50 have returned, and of those, around 12 have taken up stipendiary posts again. As far as we know, no compensation has been repaid.

This book is a collection of the reflections of 45 women priests and nine male priests and bishops in the Church of England. It also includes a chapter by the Rt Revd Penelope Jamieson, Bishop of Dunedin, New Zealand, who has written of her vision of a church in which women are equally valued and through which the healing, transformative power of God's Holy Spirit is free to blow. The women have woven their stories with intensely personal disclosure, theological reflection and sharp political observation and insight. The men have written about what having women priests as colleagues has meant to them, some of their own journeys and hopes for the future.

Donald Barnes expresses his gratitude to the women he has known and worked with, and rues the 'waste of talented people' who have had to leave because of the coldness and lack of support from their clergy colleagues. Vincent Strudwick traces his own calling and growing awareness of the rightness of women's ordination, and challenges the Church to continue with its necessary process of 'radical reshaping'.

Those who have contributed to this volume and who also voted on that day in November 1992 are Christine Farrington, Sue Hope, Patience Purchas, Judith Rose, Donald Barnes and David Hawtin. I was also on Synod then, as I am still, and I well remember walking through the door labelled 'Laity – Ayes', and the charged atmosphere of suppressed emotion.

Sue Hope was called in the debate and spoke of the 'seamless robe' of Christ's priesthood that had been flung over the *whole* body, not just part of it. The debate, she said, is not about 'whether women can become priestly or can have authority'. Rather, the debate is 'properly about whether the Church in our generation believes the social and cultural restraints which have so far inhibited women from acting as a focus for our common priesthood to have been lifted' (Report of Proceedings, General Synod November Group of Sessions 1992 23/3, p. 760).

Another speaker in the debate was June Osborne, now Canon Treasurer at Salisbury Cathedral. She addressed some of the issues that people found problematical about women priests, and ended with the statement that 'we are here today to ask whether we will test vocations. We are asking how we may allow the personality of God to be made transparent by our life together, for a calling to ordination is built on the grace of God – and I long for you to allow me to minister the grace of God through priesthood. In the mercy of Christ and for the sake of our Church, I ask you: please test my vocation.' (Report of Proceedings 23/3, pp. 724–25).

An even more impassioned speech was made by the then Bishop of Durham, David Jenkins. The debate had been going for some time, and Bishop David queried whether 'we have reached the point in this Synod, as we come near to the vote, where we have to stop being balanced in our attempts to understand and argue with one another. Ought we not perhaps rather to be broken by the shame we are bringing on God, his Christ and the Gospel? Is it not shameful to be quarrelling as we are about women in the Church when the whole world is torn by poverty, strife and lostness . . .? Is it not disgraceful that we have so little faith in the catholicity of Christ's incarnation for all and in the catholicity of the sacrament of his body and blood that we confine that sacrament to men's hands? Surely women's hands are as human and as able to be hallowed by God's grace and calling?'

Bishop David expressed anger at the possibility of the vote not passing, and observed that 'a No vote condemns us to five more years of wasted energy, and consigns called, tested and trusted women in our diaconate and elsewhere to more years of condescension and, I do honestly fear, oppression. How can we not be angry?' (Report of Proceedings 23/3, p. 764).

Others who have told their stories in this book were in the visitor's gallery or outside in Dean's Yard on that day. Newspaper articles and old photographs show familiar faces: Angela Berners-Wilson, Faith Claringbull, Rose Hudson-Wilkin, Nerissa Jones, Jean Mayland, Katharine Rumens, Fiona Stewart-Darling, Jane Tillier and David Driscoll among them. The smiles and tears speak volumes, and the sense of euphoria and release of energy still emanate from the faded cuttings.

Contexts

The ending of MOW and the beginning of WATCH

In 1990 I had been elected onto General Synod, and in June 1992 I received a telephone call from Shirley-Ann Williams, a lay member of Synod from Exeter diocese. She asked me whether I might have the time and inclination to help the Movement for the Ordination of Women with the press and media in the final run-up to the vote. Delighted, I became part of the MOW office team, although I worked mainly from home.

My closest colleague was Caroline Davies, the eminently sane and wise Executive Secretary. Caroline's quick response and fine judgement kept the campaign on track and moving forward. Jenny Standage was the indefatigable administrator who worked tirelessly in the MOW office with Caroline. Since MOW closed in 1994 I have since got to know Jenny much better as WATCH's Secretary. Jenny is one of the few remaining members of the National WATCH Committee who remembers the 'early days' of campaigning, and her experience is invaluable. Cathy Milford was the Moderator of MOW at the time, and guided us all with her gentle and inclusive way of working.

A month before the vote, Cathy engaged in a dialogue with Rowan Williams at a special MOW service in Coventry Cathedral. Rowan used the image of there being a stone in front of imagination and prayer and asked the question, 'Who will roll it away?' Cathy responded by saying:

> In my bones I feel that our particular stone, the stone of deep prejudice against women, has been rolled back. Not in the sense that there is not still plenty to be worked through, but in the sense that prejudice has been exposed for what it is. There is a clarity about the issues involved, there is an understanding that the ordination of women is not an isolated issue but that it is connected to and interwoven with the needs of the world today. There is a groundswell of understanding of the far reaching implications of the change that cannot now be stopped. (Margaret Webster, *A New Strength, A New Song*, Mowbray 1994, p. 172)

I remember so many others, not voices in this book, but

people whose involvement was crucial in the time before the vote. Margaret Webster, who was MOW's Executive Secretary from 1979 to 1986, has written the history of MOW and the campaign for women priests in her book *A New Strength, A New Song*. It should be required reading for every ordinand in the Church of England. Margaret and her husband Alan, the former Dean of St Paul's, continue to campaign for women's full inclusion in the Church.

Another inspiration was the World Health Organisation doctor and Anglican priest, Susan Cole-King, who returned from America to stand in solidarity with the English women deacons during the final stages of the campaign. Sadly Susan died last year, at the age of 66, fatally weakened by a parasite she had got while working in Africa. There were so many others then, and there are so many others now, women and men living lives of immense integrity, courage and grace.

I also remember fascinating hours spent with the indomitable Christian Howard, now departed, who befriended me and advised me on Synod strategy, and the focused and gracious Diana McClatchey, another former Moderator of MOW. There was also the incisive Monica Furlong who has contributed so much over the years. The year before the vote Monica wrote a book about women and power in the Church. She observed that 'most of us began the campaign with fairly simple ideas about what it was we were trying to do, and only gradually perceived the enormity of it. Attempting modestly to catch a small fish – that is, to get women ordained – we were astounded to discover that we had got Leviathan at the end of the line, that unwittingly we had reached into the very depths of the malaise not merely of the Church but of society itself'(Monica Furlong, *A Dangerous Delight*, SPCK 1991, p. 11). I am very aware, as are many of the contributors to this book, that we are still discovering the true nature of that Leviathan.

Another friend and fellow-worker that I met around the time of the vote and who has been a staunch supporter, first of MOW and more recently of WATCH, is David Lloyd. He and his wife Muriel, no longer alive, have campaigned for women's full inclusion in the Church for well over half a century. It is thanks to David that so much has been possible, especially over the last few years.

It was decided in 1994 to close down MOW. Between March and July of that year all of the 1,500 deacons who had felt called to be priests had been ordained. MOW was a single-issue campaign group, and its mission had been accomplished. Not everyone agreed that MOW should fold, but at a meeting with the Central Council and all the diocesan representatives a straw poll was taken, and it was decided to bring what had been a very successful group to an end. I can even remember being asked to speak at a National Association of Women's Organisations (NAWO) meeting, when NAWO still existed. Though a secular organization, it wanted to hear how MOW had run such a successful campaign. The voices that warned us that we should keep the MOW network healthy and intact for the inevitable work of the future lost to those that urged us to honour our original objective. And so MOW closed.

The office was packed up and Caroline, Jenny and I ceased to be paid. It was clear that many of the people who had been involved with MOW were tired and needed to get back to the rest of their lives. But, as Jenny and I discovered, most of the press and media and universities and schools did not know that MOW did not exist any more. There was a steady and growing interest in wider society in these new creatures, women priests, and the extra phone line that I had installed in 1992 kept on ringing. Brenda Wolfe, an MOW member who had faithfully sent off MOW fact packs to requests from students kept having to send off the packs.

Jenny and I carried on responding to all the letters and telephone calls, becoming increasingly aware that we had entered a new phase. More calls started to come from ordained women who wanted to talk about something that was happening to them in their parishes. Did it seem reasonable that their incumbent had said this or done that? Were they being paranoid about not being told, yet again, about a certain meeting or service? How should they respond to critical or offensive comments and behaviour?

MOW had achieved its aim, but the work of integrating women priests into the Church was only beginning. Of course, in many, if not most parishes things were going smoothly. The women, who had all been deacons and experienced ministers, were already accepted, and their priesting only served to draw them and their congregations closer together. The problems were mainly with fellow clergy, and some clergy wives, and with others in the Church hierarchy.

Caroline Davies, Jean Mayland, Donald and Sally Barnes and others met to discuss what should be done. It was decided that a new group would have to be created, a group that would monitor how women priests were being treated and that would begin to campaign for women bishops.

In London, such a group called Women and the Church (WATCH) had already been formed. It knew well that with the level of antagonism towards women priests in some areas a support and monitoring body was essential. A small working party drew up the constitution and aims of National WATCH, and on 9 November 1996 National WATCH came into existence. Its aims were to work for women bishops, for a more honest and transparent system of appointments, and for the end of all discrimination in the Church of England.

The wording on the front of the new WATCH leaflets stated that 'WATCH has a vision of the Church of England as a community of God's people where justice and equality prevail. WATCH believes that this vision is rooted in the Scriptures and enfolds God's will for the whole world.'

I was elected as WATCH's first Chair, with Jenny as Secretary and another General Synod and MOW stalwart, Marion Simpson, as Treasurer. About 12 others were elected to the committee, and we made our base in St John's Church, Waterloo, at the invitation of the rector, Richard Truss, and the curate, Katharine Rumens.

The next spring, on 10 May 1997, WATCH held its inaugural service at St Martin-in-the-Fields, thanks to the vicar, Nick Holtam, and with the help of Clare Herbert and Mandy Hodgson. Susan Cole-King preached, and hundreds of purple and gold balloons festooned the portico of the church.

Over the next few years WATCH groups began in dioceses around the country. It had been decided not to reconstitute MOW's formal structure, with diocesan representatives, office and paid employees. WATCH would have a lighter structure, and encourage regional groups to respond to their own issues, with help from the centre as and when needed.

The Act of Synod

Almost exactly a year to the day after the vote on women priests, General Synod passed an Act of Synod that is without historical precedent. The Act allowed for the creation of a new kind of ecclesiastical creature – the flying bishop. These men would be deployed to provide episcopal support and pastoral care for clergy and laity who could not accept such care from their own bishops. They would be a pastoral extension of the diocesan bishop. These special bishops were to be known officially as PEVs, Provincial Episcopal Visitors, visiting with the permission and blessing of the diocesan bishops in both provinces of the Church of England.

Further, PCCs could vote to place their parishes in the care of a PEV under a new resolution, Resolution C. The two Resolutions, A and B, in the Women Priests Measure did not provide enough 'safeguards' for some of those opposed to women's ordination. It was not enough to be able to refuse to have a visiting woman celebrant or a woman incumbent; a new Act was needed to ensure that traditionalist clergy would not have to minister alongside a bishop who was in favour of women priests, and who may have laid hands on a woman to ordain her, thus becoming 'tainted' with irregularity.

Very quickly, bad practice flourished in new ways under the Act. A woman priest was offered a post in a parish, only to be telephoned three days later by the bishop and told that she 'hadn't got the job because the church warden wouldn't work with a woman'. The convictions of one opposing church warden were permitted to overturn the decision of the parish as a whole. Would this have happened with no Act of Synod? A retired priest refused to take a service at a nearby church because a woman had celebrated at the altar. Would this have been catered for without the Act of Synod? In one diocese, the bishop gave permission to traditionalist clergy to conduct their own services at the diocesan clergy conference, an event supposedly designed to bring the clergy of the diocese together for thought, prayer and worship. In another diocese, a male priest was approved unanimously by a multi-parish benefice that included a traditionalist parish, only to be asked at the last moment not to take up the post because one of the flying bishops had alerted the parish that the man was not opposed to women priests. There are many other similar tales.

I wrote in my submission to the Review Group set up to see how the Act was working, that, in spite of all these stories, 'if I were to name what I believe is the greatest harm done by the Act, it would be the creation of a new climate in which it was felt to be permissible to discriminate openly against women and to voice clear prejudice against women. Much of the ministry of the flying bishops is a tacit acknowledgement that the Church of England still colludes with a debased view of women.'

Not only does the Act provide for 'pure' hands to minister to those who do not accept the priestly ministry of women, it has also developed into providing untainted hands for those who do not accept the ministry of male bishops who ordain and work with female colleagues. Judith Maltby comments in her chapter in *Act of Synod – Act of Folly?* 'at no point in our history has the endorsement of comprehensiveness ever resulted in the creation of an extended or alternative episcopal system' (Monica Furlong, *Act of Synod – Act of Folly?*, SCM Press 1998, p. 51). Judith goes on to observe that 'your bishop can deny the resurrection, the Trinity, and the incarnation; he may be a racist, liar or thief – but no one will offer you a PEV. But if he ordains a woman to the priesthood, you can call in a "safe pair of hands"' (*Act of Synod – Act of Folly?*, p. 56).

The Review Group, chaired by the Bishop of Blackburn, produced its Report in 2000, to be debated in Synod in July. News leaked that the bishops themselves had rejected a first report as being too much of a whitewash. The Report that emerged was still a whitewash: almost all critical references to the Act had been expunged. The hundreds of letters sent in describing discrimination and bad practice had vanished from the final Report. Anyone new to the scene who read the Report would have come away with the distinct impression that the Act was a jolly good thing doing sterling work in keeping the Church together following women's ordinations. The only really beneficial effect the Report had was to debunk the use of the phrase, the 'two integrities'. People could hold differing views about women with integrity, but, of course, it was a nonsense to speak of 'two integrities'. Apart from that helpful clarification, very little else described the true attitude towards the Act. The tone of the

Report and its implicit editorial stance suggested a Church that was reluctant to accept women's priestly ministry.

The Revd Valerie Bonham, speaking in the debate on the Report in General Synod, voiced her concern. 'Now we are being called into question, not just by those who in conscience cannot accept our ministry but by those very bishops who have encouraged us, affirmed us and ordained us . . . That is incredibly undermining, not only of us as priests in the Church of God but of us as human beings made in the image of God' (Report of Proceedings 31/2, p. 118).

When Dr Helen Thorne wrote up her study of the first women priests in the Church of England, she concluded that the Act of Synod is

> deeply harmful to women on a practical, emotional and spiritual level. The Act of Synod, and the provision of alternative Episcopal oversight, are offensive to women because they legitimise women's exclusion and create a form of sexual apartheid by creating areas in the Church where women's ministry is unacceptable. Emotionally, women are damaged by the constant sense of rejection, unworthiness and the abusive behaviour that the Act can generate. Spiritually, the Act fosters a theology of 'taint' whereby a man's ministry is made void through his association with a woman priest. In a binary, dualistic view of sexual difference, the Act legitimises male spirituality, whilst it denies women's acceptability before God and denigrates their ministry . . . The Church cannot maintain its theological integrity, nor can it be a credible voice in society if it fails to rid itself of this divisive legislation. (Helen Thorne, *Journey to Priesthood*, CCSRG Monograph Series 3, Department of Theology and Religious Studies, University of Bristol, 2000)

The birth of GRAS

As WATCH began to grow, so did an increasing anger at the abuses done to women priests in the name of the Act of Synod. In October 2000 a new group was launched, a new single issue group – GRAS – the Group for Rescinding the Act of Synod, with the Revd Mary Robins, Honorary Curate at St James, Piccadilly, as its national co-ordinator. Former MOW activists, members of the Modern Churchpeople's Union and WATCH members banded together to 'draw attention to the strength of prejudice against women in the Church of England' and to motivate the bishops to 'give women clergy the unambiguous and un-equivocal support they deserve'.

Baronness Ruth Rendell arranged for GRAS to have its launch in a room in the House of Lords, and Martyn Percy and I were asked to give the inaugural speeches. GRAS gained rapid support from people who were incensed with how the Act of Synod was being worked and, more seriously, by what the Act implied about women.

In November 2001, just two months after the terrorist attack on the World Trade Centre, Anthony Howard wrote an article about the Act of Synod in *The Times*. He had attended a GRAS event and was outraged by the way the Act was operating in the Church. 'In appeasing prejudice', he wrote, 'it legitimised it. The whole aim of the Act was to demonstrate that both clergy and laity could continue to resist the introduction of women priests with just as much "integrity" – the favoured buzzword – as applied to those who sought to bring the already approved meas-ure into practice. There could hardly have been a worse example of weedy Anglican compromise.' Howard ended the article with a pithy challenge: 'A week that saw the fall of the Taleban is not a bad moment for the C of E to end sexual discrimination' (*The Times*, 20 November 2001).

My feelings about the debate in Synod when the Act was first brought before us are now those of having been conned. The then Archbishop of York, John Habgood, presented the Act as the only Christian way to proceed. It is not surprising that only a handful of Synod members spoke or voted against the Act. The bishops had bonded on this one, and nothing was going to derail their solution of keeping the small number of their brothers on board who would otherwise have felt it necessary to leave the Church.

I had gone to Manchester in January 1993 when the bishops made a statement to the press about the Act of Synod. Returning to the train station, I shared a cab with one of the bishops. 'How long do you think the Act will last?' I asked him, aware that at the press conference it had been stated that the Act was here to stay. 'Oh, about 15 years – or less' was his reply. He may just prove to be right.

Moving towards women bishops

In 1986 a group called the Archbishops' Group on the Episcopate was formed with a remit to consider 'the nature and function of the episcopate in the Church, including a particular examination of the theological issues bearing upon the ordination of women to the episcopate'. Their Report, running to nearly 350 pages, discussed at length the various practices and traditions of the past and tried to look into the future. I am amazed that all that rigorous thought and study has dated so quickly that it has been necessary to engage in a similar exercise all over again with the current House of Bishops Working Party on the Theology of Women in the Episcopate.

Even then, the Archbishops' Group cited another House of Bishops Report that had concluded: 'It is very difficult to sustain an argument for any essential sacramental distinction between the presbyterate and the episcopate such as to put in doubt the possibility of a woman's admission to the episcopate once the presbyterate has been granted.' In other words, once women can be priests, they should also be able to be bishops.

By the late 1990s it seemed that the best way forward was for someone to put a motion before General Synod, to test Synod's mind about the consecration of women as bishops. Lambeth Conference had taken place that year, with its inclusion of 11 female bishops from the United States, Canada and New Zealand. The media had taken to these bishops, and they were even asked to pose for a special photograph. The result was a colourful picture of the 11 women taken outdoors in bright sunshine, robed in red and white, poised, smiling and confident, with a magnificent view of Canterbury Cathedral in the distance. The experience of having the women bishops here, with some preaching and lecturing as well as giving interviews, helped to make the idea of having women bishops in the Church of England seem more of a reality.

After a great deal of discussion, the Archdeacon of Tonbridge, the Venerable Judith Rose, agreed to propose a Private Members

Motion. In July 2000, the General Synod debated and passed her
motion, which reads:

> That this Synod ask the House of Bishops to initiate further
> theological study on the episcopate, focussing on the issues
> that need to be addressed in preparation for the debate on
> women in the episcopate in the Church of England, and to
> make a progress report on this study to Synod in the next two
> years.

While I would have preferred the word 'progress' not to have
been included, I was delighted that Judith was willing to initiate
the Synodical process with this motion. At the Synod meeting in
July of this year, the working party, chaired by the Bishop of
Rochester, Michael Nazir-Ali, gave its progress report and out-
lined its longer-term plans.

Earlier this year a small group drawn together by WATCH
had been invited to meet with the working party in person. We
learned that on the same day, 'Forward in Faith', the umbrella
group for Anglo-Catholic traditionalists, had also met with the
working party. The impression that can sometimes be given by
those in the Church and also by journalists who, quite rightly,
strive to get both sides of the story, is that opinion is roughly
divided between the two camps. It is not. The real picture is
much closer to a 90 per cent versus 10 per cent, not the 50–50
division that can be implied. This knowledge only makes the
tortuous pace of the working party more difficult to accept. The
working party, in its written submission to accompany its
progress report to Synod, disclosed that at its first meeting it was
agreed that:

> The work should be in three stages. Firstly, an examination of
> the theology of the episcopate. Secondly, on the basis of that
> theology, to ask whether it was right to have women bishops.
> Thirdly, to address the issue of communion and the impair-
> ment of communion, if the Church was to ordain women to
> the episcopate. (*Working Party on the Episcopate: A Progress
> Report from the House of Bishops*, GS 1457, Archbishops'
> Council 2002, p. 2)

We know from other writings that Bishop Michael Nazir-Ali has concluded that, for himself, there are no theological objections to women bishops, just practical ones. The problem is centred on priests who will feel unable to belong to a 'college' of priests with a woman at its head. As Jane Shaw and others have already pointed out elsewhere, if he believes there to be no theological objections, then any remaining objections boil down to discrimination.

We heard this type of reasoning in 1975 when General Synod decided that there was 'no fundamental objection' to the ordination of women to the priesthood, and yet it took another 17 years to come to the decisive vote. In terms of process, we have been here before. The question is, how much longer can the Church spin out the process of consecrating women as bishops in a Church that is overwhelmingly looking forward to their ministry?

Things are changing. There are cracks in the dam. Guildford Diocesan Synod passed a motion in June 2001 that 'asks that the General Synod bring forward legislation to permit the consecration of women to the Episcopate in the provinces of Canterbury and York without delay'. This motion now joins the queue of other diocesan motions to be debated by General Synod, but even if it takes a few years, it will still be helpful in moving the process forward. As Anne Foreman, a member of General Synod from Guildford, wrote in her speech to Guildford Diocesan Synod, 'I believe preparation for legislation needs to go hand in hand with preparation for the debate on women bishops. Otherwise the work of the Rochester Working Party will be in danger of being perceived as a delaying mechanism, with potentially divisive consequences.'

Martyn Percy believes that the 'heart of the dilemma for those who are charged with coming to a common mind in the near future about women bishops is the identity of the Church of England, its theological methodologies and authorities'. Martyn goes on to argue that the very nature, history and tradition of the Church is plural, and as such, 'there is no one 'right' tradition that makes up Anglicanism'.

However long it takes to prepare the legislation for women bishops, one thing must not be compromised. There must be no qualifying legislation that distinguishes between bishops on the basis of sex. A bishop is a bishop, full stop. There must be no new Act of Synod, qualifying the authority and ministry of bishops who happen to be female. Although so many are eager to have women bishops, this is one of the principles that must be agreed and reflected in the legislation.

Are women still seen as a problem?

That discriminatory views against women continue to exist in the Church, and also in society, would suggest that there are strong underlying systems of thought perpetuating such views. At this stage in the history and development of humankind negative attitudes and behaviour towards women cannot be explained by ignorance or default. Collectively, the Church must still be actively adhering to these views, and finding successful ways of passing them on to each new generation.

There are so many different explanations about how and why the rot set in: some theologians hark back to Genesis, and suggest that if Genesis 1:27 is considered normative and definitive, and not the account in Genesis 2, then to value female human beings differently than male human beings is to desecrate God's intended relationship with humanity and distort God's will for how female and male humans are to relate. These theologians argue that there never was intended to be a hierarchy between the sexes in the human species, and that part of the significance and purpose of Jesus' life and death was to heal the disorder between women and men.

Paul's prohibitions about women have also determined how women have been treated in many churches throughout Christian history. The most important thing for Paul is that he knew himself and all Christians to be 'discharged from the law, dead to that which held us captive, so that we serve not under the old written code but in the new life of the Spirit' (Romans 7:6). It seems that Paul occasionally reverted into a former way of thinking, and that he was also writing specific instructions to specific churches at a specific time in history. Taking his writings as a whole, I am most struck by his passion for the saving, liberating, transcendent love of Christ, not by his quibbles with what women, as opposed to men, should or should not be doing.

Other theologians place part of the blame on the influence of

Greek philosophical dualism. In that system things were divided into pairs of opposites, such as light/dark, wet/dry, hot/cold, good/evil, mind/emotions and spirit/body. One of these pairs was male/female. Not only were these pairs seen as opposites, the different halves of the pairs were invested with different value. So, for instance, the mind was valued over and against the emotions. The spirit was valued over the body, and so on. To make matters worse, certainly for women, the mind and spirit were associated with the male, and the emotions and body were associated with the female – along with other characteristics and qualities of which every good Christian man was trying to rid himself!

Added to this dualistic approach to reality, Aristotle's understanding of biology was prevalent in the last few centuries leading up to the start of Christianity and beyond. It was later adopted into medieval scholasticism, and wasn't entirely refuted until the modern era. Even up until the Enlightenment most scientists were still relying on the work of Aristotle and others who taught that women were imperfect versions of men. (For more on this issue, read Jane Shaw's chapter in *Act of Synod – Act of Folly?*)

It was also believed that only males created new life, and further, that masculinity was the norm. Women were only incubators for the complete male seed and, in an ideal world, all humans were intended to be male. However, sometimes things went wrong – there was a foul easterly wind or the pregnant woman was foolish enough to sit on damp ground, and so some humans were born female. Aquinas even called women 'misbegotten men'. Did these worthy thinkers never wonder about what would happen if everything went 'right', thereby eventually doing away with all the incubators?

The Christian feminist theologian Rosemary Radford Ruether considers that the role of dualism still affects our understanding of the nature of God, and she contends that 'seeing nature and transcendence, matter and spirit as female against male is basic to male theology' (Rosemary Radford Ruether, *Feminist Theology* 21, May 1999, p. 102).

Perhaps one of the more enlightening facts about how women were viewed is the record of a minor council that met in the fourth century. The clever and good Christian men of the day were set to debate, among other things, the question 'Are women human?' History records that the council decided, with two votes over a simple majority, that women *were* human.

Also in the fourth century the brilliant but tormented Augustine disagreed with his contemporaries about whether women could bear the image of God. Somewhat radically, he concluded that they could, but only in their minds and spirits, not, of course, in their bodies. Unlike men, women's bodies made them, on their own, unable to bear the image of God.

We would like to think that that type of thinking had vanished in the dim and distant past, but some of the comments made to women, and to men, in the last ten years show that a debased view of women and their bodies still persists at the beginning of the third millennium.

We can grimace or laugh now at the writings of some of the Church Fathers, otherwise holy and thoughtful people, who made their views about women all too clear. Tertullian, writing in the later part of the first and the early second century, asserted that 'women are the gateway to the devil'. The great letter writer, Jerome, considered, among other things, that 'woman is a temple built over a sewer'. Odo of Cluny, a pious abbot of the tenth century, was of the opinion that 'to embrace a woman is to embrace a sack of manure'. (For more about traditional views of women, read Elaine Storkey's *Contributions to Christian Feminism*, Christian Impact 1995.)

The laughter, however, becomes somewhat more hollow in response to similar comments made within the last ten years. In 1995 a male Anglican priest who had decided to become a Roman Catholic said to a Catholic nun, 'I'd rather ordain a cat than a woman.' A few years earlier another male Anglican priest was heard to pronounce, 'You can no more ordain a woman than you can ordain a pork pie!' Such comments give women the status of a different species, so we are back to the fourth century, it seems.

Although most of the women's voices minimize this phenomenon, it has been a feature of life for many ordained women. From the dozens of anecdotes I have heard over the years, many women priests are made to carry burdens on behalf of all womankind. Their bodies, sexuality and reproductive systems are often considered to be more integral to what they bring to their priestly ministry than those of their male counterparts. During interviews and at other times women are often asked questions about their sexuality that few, if any, men are ever asked.

Hurtful and ridiculous comments aside, this is not entirely negative. It's about time that priests, male and female, were encouraged to integrate their sexuality and their priesthood. Part of the problem has been, of course, a false and damaging separation of role and person, priest and human being. It is unfair on the women, but it is heartening that one of the ramifications of including women in the priesthood has been an opening up of this whole area. Simply by being who they are, which includes being female, women are beginning to help some people to re-integrate their sexuality and spirituality.

But the issue, in much more subtle form, persists, perhaps most succinctly summed up by Una Kroll's challenge before the vote: 'Either ordain us or don't baptize us.' Either women are full members of the body of Christ, or they are not. Either women are included in the saving, transforming, liberating, reconciling work of Jesus Christ, or they are not. Either God's Holy Spirit is given to women as it is to men, or it is not. The question lingers: Are women fully human in the eyes of the Church? The current Interim Report on the Structure and Funding of Ordination Training from the Ministry Division of the Archbishops' Council states that 'ministry is the transforming grace of God' and emphasizes that ministry belongs to Christ, and if 'we seek to participate in and embody a ministry which belongs to Christ himself we can only pursue the highest standards of faithfulness of discipleship, spiritual wisdom, commitment to common life and deep wells of motivation . . . we will guard against incompetencies and complacencies which undermine the creativity and harmony of the whole people of God' (p. 23).

If these are the true goals, then I cannot imagine the Church ever being able to realize them if it does not value women equally with men, explicitly, in its structures and orders, and also in the implicit messages it sends out about women. I also think the Church will fail to achieve these goals if it does not learn to value and empower the laity in new ways. If the purpose of ministry really is the 'transforming grace of God' that is brought about through a way of relating to the whole people of God, then there is still much work to do before we achieve that purpose.

Listening to the voices

In November 1992, some of those who have contributed to this volume were barely out of their teens: Helen Duckett and Rachel Wood were both born in 1971, and Jane Haslam in 1970. At the other end of the age range, three of the contributors were born in the 1920s. Most of the voices are of those who had been waiting, those who had already been deaconed, and who took their place among the first 1,500 women to be priested in 1994.

We hear from those in rural, urban and suburban settings, parish priests, university lecturers, those in some form of chaplaincy and those who have retired. Una Kroll now lives as a solitary in a life of prayer. We have sought voices from the north, south, east and west. We hear from some who grew up in the United States and who now live and minister in England, bringing a different and valuable perspective. We include a chapter from the only British woman who is also a bishop, Penelope Jamieson, Bishop of Dunedin in New Zealand. We have attempted to gather voices that span the entire spectrum of churchmanship, from the Anglo-Catholic to the Evangelical, with a wide variety of shadings and positions in between.

We took the decision not to arrange the submissions alphabetically or chronologically, but to try to order them in some way that gives shape to the narrative of the past ten years. Inevitably, many of the voices make reference to the day of the vote, and memories of 11 November 1992 have been significant for both women and men. Also, many contain thoughts about the future. In addition to those common threads, it has been possible to see themes and sense direction, and the order hopefully reflects movement and progression, with some of the voices grouped around a common theme, such as motherhood.

What has been impossible, however, is to gather the entire breadth of ordained women in the Church of England; for that we would have needed submissions from all of the 2,100 women priests. This book can only be a small, but hopefully rich and rewarding taste of some of what women have brought to the priesthood. There is also the ecumenical context: as I write we are preparing to hear how the Anglican–Methodist conversations are progressing. We know that the Methodist Church has made it clear that its stance on women is non-negotiable. It will not agree to formal unity until and unless the Church of England opens the episcopate to women.

In regard to the Roman Catholic Church, it was announced recently that six women were ordained priests on a barge in Amsterdam! If a Roman Catholic bishop now officially acknowledges their priestly status, then could the Roman Catholic Church be accepting women priests as part of a grassroots movement?

Some of the voices we do hear in this book are single, some widowed and some married, with and without children. The experience of motherhood has featured prominently in several contributions, and for many has proved to be tremendously positive – a strong bond for these priests and their parishioners who are also mothers.

Some priests have written of how people find them approachable because they are a 'mum' like them. Emma Percy comments that as a mother, 'I have found it a wonderful job to combine with bringing up my children . . . My mothering and my ministry are collaborative and I am able to bring vision, shape and leadership to both roles.'

Helen Duckett observes of herself and other priests who are mothers, that 'Sharing the common female experience of childbearing and childbirth helped to remove them from their spiritual priestly pedestal, and put them on an equal footing with "normal" women . . . Such responses obviously raise huge questions about the stereotypes and expectations that surround issues of gender and sexuality, and understandings of the identities and roles of women and men both in the Church and in the wider world.'

Other voices speak of the problems that pregnancy has brought, the worry of whether their parishioners' enthusiasm for them would turn to something else once they realised that the vicar would be taking maternity leave. There are also observations about the different attitudes towards priests who are mothers and priests who are fathers.

The most poignant and moving accounts have spoken of the shadow side of pregnancy and motherhood. These, shared by a number of women, include stories of childlessness and of miscarriage. Jane Tillier tells that once while she was pregnant, she was asked to hold the stillborn baby girl of one of her parishioners, and later to conduct her funeral: 'Her parents explain that they feel able to ask me to do all this, even mindful of my rounded belly, because they know my story of repeated miscarriage.' During the editing of this book, Jane telephoned me to say that she had just had another miscarriage – her sixth. The effects of this type of experience, that of intense emotional, and, at times, physical pain, have made powerful connections with other women in ways not fully anticipated or imagined when the vote was passed.

Seventeen of the women who have contributed are half of a clergy couple, and some of their reflections raise issues that the Church has yet to address. Wendy Bracegirdle believes that there is 'much to explore in the richness of married priesthood, more to be described than a facile, oversimplified thesis of complementarity'. She also comments wryly that 'many bishops seem mystified by the new phenomenon, ill-equipped to recognise rich potential, readier to anticipate problems and quite unable to understand a couple as one unity and yet two persons'.

Many ordained women, not only those who have contributed to this book, have spoken of a strong, clear sense of having been called to the priesthood, some from a very early age, even before it was possible to test that calling. Some tell of responding, often hesitantly at first, to a call that initially seemed illogical or improbable. Others tell of receiving the call after they had already spent years in another career or after they had married and had children.

Jane Bass recounts how she was driving home one day 'when a still quiet voice said audibly, "I want you to be a priest." I was nearly paralysed with shock and pulled into the nearest coffee shop for a stiff black coffee and to consider what manner of request this was or whether I had gone dotty in the hot sun . . . here I was at 29, happily married with two small children, being told to do the impossible. Surely God was joking!' From this type of response Jane, and others like her, moved to a joyous acceptance of what they knew God was asking of them.

Flora Winfield experienced an altogether different call. From a childhood sense of loneliness, alienation and difference, and through an intense awareness of other people's hidden pain, she writes that, for her, 'the experience of vocation has been about weakness: and it has always felt as if that which is most broken in me is that which is most called'.

Over and over again women exhibit the qualities of humility, good humour, self-awareness and the ability to live with tension, ambiguity and hostility. They express immense generosity of spirit and person in how they have accommodated those who have not been able to accommodate them. They are all too conscious that they minister in a Church, typically with a high degree of loyalty and grace, that still examines their priesthood in a way that it does not examine the priesthood of men. Their analysis of their own situations is remarkably perceptive but, in spite of the many injustices and indignities they have endured, they display a remarkable lack of bitterness or rancour.

At a recent Consultation at St George's House, Windsor Castle, two of the female North American bishops attended, Victoria Matthews from Canada and Geralyn Wolf from the United States. Their response to aspects of the current situation for women in the Church of England, in particular some of the behaviour that hides under the dirty mac of the Act of Synod, was almost incredulity. They saw the ordained women in the Church as brave, strong, long-suffering and gracious beyond belief.

The stories reveal a Church that is still biased towards the male, still discriminatory against the female, one that still condones or colludes with behaviour and attitudes which would relegate women to a second place in ministry and, at times, it seems even to a second order of creation. There is still talk of women's priestly ministry waiting to be fully 'received' by the Church, without an agreed definition of what 'received' might mean. At a variety of gatherings over the past few months I have heard women affirming that they know their priestly ministry already to have been 'received' by the Church. More and more, women, and many men too, are refusing to use the language of reception about women's ordinations any more. For some, the vote in 1992 demonstrated that women priests were received by the Church, for others, the overall welcome women have been given is proof that their priestly ministry has been accepted.

Nerissa Jones and others make the point that by ordaining women the Church sent the message that it stopped thinking of women as lesser creatures. Ordination is not, and should not be, necessary to determine or affirm the goodness of men or of women, but by ordaining women there was the strong sense that women were being affirmed and accepted as women in a new way.

The dissonance between the theologians and the holy men of their day who contributed valuable thinking to the developing understanding of the Christian faith, but who, at the same time, produced comments about women which revealed a debased attitude towards half the human race. Inability to distinguish between Christian teaching and doctrine and culturally determined views has produced a faith that, so often and in so many places, implies a view of women human beings as lesser than male human beings.

The typical response I get as I travel around England speaking to a wide variety of groups, organizations and institutions is one of outrage: how dare women be treated in such a way! How dare the women and those who believe that women should share in the ordained priesthood put up with it! How dare the Church get away with such demeaning and discriminating behaviour!

After one lecture at a university, during the discussion time, a young woman in the audience kept on asking questions, the type of raw questions that I, and most people who have worked in and around the Church for some time, have ceased to ask. It was refreshing and somewhat shaming to realize how much we now accept, and how appalling and unacceptable it all seems to someone who has not been enculturated into the Church of England.

Even when I speak at theological colleges to people who, one might suppose, should know more about the Church than most, I often encounter an uncomprehending audience once they hear of the Act of Synod, the Financial Provisions in the Women Priests Measure, and even Resolutions A and B.

The next step, ordaining women as bishops will be a sign to the Church and the rest of society, and do not think that society is not watching and waiting for such a sign, that women are valued as much as men are valued. Of course, it will be perhaps another generation or two before women are deployed primarily for their gifts and experience, without a disproportionately heightened awareness of their sex.

We need to think carefully about what we want. Do we want a church that has females doing what males have been doing for centuries, or a church that is willing to become something new as it incorporates a fuller humanity, a more well-rounded perspective and experience?

In time, the concept of a God who we say we believe is neither male nor female, and who we say we believe includes both our femininity and masculinity, will be more genuinely understood and accepted. The strong resistance to, even fear of, inclusive language should moderate over time as people see women presiding at the Eucharist, taking part in Maundy Thursday foot-washing services, and in all the other roles traditionally taken only by men.

Ann Nickson experienced a moment of insight as she took the role of Jesus for the long Palm Sunday reading from St Matthew's Gospel. 'As a woman, reading those words of Jesus, suddenly I understood for the first time why the thought of a woman at the altar is so problematic for some; at the same time I realized why it was so important, not just for women, but for all human beings, that a woman should stand before God at the altar. That because Christ shared our common humanity as women and men, because his cry of forsakenness sums up the cries of all the God-forsaken men, women and children throughout the world and throughout the ages, that same common humanity as women and men should be presented to God in the Eucharist.'

Women will have to continue to stand against the particular demons that attack the feminine in this culture: low self-esteem, the necessity of being 'nice' above all else, of being pliant, always accommodating, self-effacing. Women are already having to get accustomed to being considered unreasonable when they stick up for themselves or for their ideas, of being called overbearing when they take an equally active part in discussions and meetings with their male colleagues, and of being considered hard when they respond to situations and people with a degree of firmness and decisiveness.

Christine Farrington recounts the story of receiving an Easter card this year from her suffragan bishop with a cartoon of five men and one woman seated around a table during a meeting. The chairman is speaking: 'That's an excellent suggestion, Miss Triggs. Perhaps one of the men here would like to make it.' Christine comments that the fact that her bishop could send her such a card gave her great hope!

One woman priest I know, very senior in her diocese, was having a private, professional conversation with her bishop about two other ordained women in the diocese who were in danger of falling out with each other. During the course of the conversation, the bishop became visibly irritated with having to deal with the particular pastoral issues between the two clergy. He burst out, 'People wanted women ordained, and this is what we get!'

With so many men it seems to be a head–heart divide. Bishops who ordain women and other male priests who are supposedly in favour of women's ordinations, do strange things like appoint a 'Forward in Faith' Diocesan Director of Ordinands, or ask women not to touch a certain man during an ordination service, for fear of 'taint', or collude with a whole list of discourteous, offensive and harmful behaviour. The weaker sex, it seems, is routinely expected by the Church to shoulder much greater burdens of discrimination and bad treatment, while showing a much greater ability to forgive, absorb, build bridges and rise above such treatment. In short, women are expected and are relied upon to exhibit much greater personal, spiritual and psychological strength.

John Saxbee reflects that 'perhaps we will only be fully a whole and healthy church when a woman priest can go ill, or astray, or slightly dotty without women's ministry as a whole being thereby diminished – as if male clergy didn't just occasionally fall victim to these all too human experiences!'

Many of the issues that women priests face are the same, of course, for women in other professions. A few years ago, when a small delegation from National WATCH met with Joan Ruddock, the then Minister for Women, she remarked how familiar-sounding the dynamics and problems for women in the Church sounded. She said that we could have been describing the position of women in the government.

We need now to prepare for the next phase, the gradual becoming of a Church that includes both women and men at all levels of its ordained ministry. It will not be enough to slot the women in to the system and assume that the result will be a renewed and transformed Church.

The Reverend John Bell of the Iona Community said to me during a conversation we were having at the Greenbelt Arts Festival in 1996 that if we want to discover what women will bring to the Church and if we want the Church to reflect both women's and men's thinking about God, then all men should keep silent for 30 years! Only then would we have a chance of learning what differences women bring to our faith and tradition. It is a lovely thought in one sense; let the women do the theology for a generation, and then see what has changed.

In the wake of the Stephen Lawrence inquiry, the Church began to tackle its own racism. The then Bishop of Stepney, John Sentamu, now Bishop of Birmingham, was an advisor for the Stephen Lawrence Inquiry, and he presented a report to the General Synod. The Church admitted that it was institutionally rascist, and put into action a programme of racism awareness training, starting with the Archbishops' Council. Some of the questions asked in regard to the Church and racism are also relevant when asked about women.

Is the Church a place of haven for women? Is the Church modelling best practice in treating women with respect and honour? Is it including women at every level of its life? I believe that the Church will have to undergo a similar programme of gender awareness training if we are to combat effectively the insidious and pernicious presence of sexism still active in our Church.

Eradicating sexism will bring a new experience of wholeness to both women and men. Rosalind Brown makes the point that by having women priests there is already a new dimension for the people of God. 'We can forget that the ordination of women gives a reciprocal gift to men: the gift that was previously exclusive to women of receiving priestly ministry from people of the other gender.'

In contrast to the walls imagined by Peter Geldard, precious walls destroyed by ordaining women, Philippa Boardman reminds us of the radical inclusivity in the book of Acts, an inclusivity that transcended walls of division. The ordination of women has already broken down some walls that divided people, and women's priestly ministry has begun to draw in many who had previously felt themselves excluded by the Church.

The long, arduous journey towards women's ordination that took place during the last century is brilliantly traced by Monica Furlong in *A Dangerous Delight*. The book documents some of the more recent outlandish pronouncements about women, and I am continually struck by the resonances with historical writings. If we think we have moved beyond men thinking of women as more identified with their sexuality than men, we need to think again!

Monica writes of an Archbishops' Commission that met in 1935, with the subject of ordaining women to the priesthood on its agenda. All the fine minds on the Commission concluded that it would be wrong to ordain women. Their deep theological reasons were stated thus: 'We believe that it would be impossible for the male members of the average Anglican congregation to be present at a service at which a woman ministered without becoming unduly conscious of her sex' (Monica Furlong, *A Dangerous Delight*, p. 95).

It is heartening to realize that only nine years after that Commission sat, in 1944, Bishop R.O. Hall of Hong Kong and South China ordained the first Anglican women priest – Florence Li Tim-Oi. One of the voices in this volume is Christopher Hall, the bishop's son, and his submission takes the form of a letter to his father. Of course, both Bishop Hall and Florence Li Tim-Oi suffered because of their action, but it was done and, after many trials and tribulations, Florence was eventually allowed to minister openly as a priest.

The voices contained in this book, and the voices of so many others, are of those who continue to live and work and hope for wholeness. They, and people of faith the world over, continue to keep fresh and alive the vision of the kingdom of God, a kingdom of justice and mercy, mutuality and service, giving and receiving, dignity, worth, joy and freedom, compassion and love. This is the vision to which they are called – this is the vision to which they remain true.

Part Two

Listening to the Voices

Priesthood and Womanhood: Questions and Answers

UNA KROLL

By the time I became a priest in January 1997, I had passed the retiring age for clergy in the Church in Wales to which I then belonged. Ordination was the culmination of a 50-year struggle to admit to myself that women could become priests in the Anglican Church, then, with others, to work to convince the Church that they would be an asset to the ordained ministry. By the time it became possible for women in the Church in Wales to be ordained, I knew many women bishops and priests from overseas, and women priests from England, and I had seen many of them in action.

At the time I was perplexed by the English and Welsh churches' insistence on restricting women's ministry, so perplexed that I seriously considered not offering for ordination myself. However, I wanted to know how female priests could make positive contributions to a Church that had been dominated by male ministry for nearly 2,000 years. I knew that I wanted to explore that potential from inside the ordained ministry rather than from outside; so I agreed to go ahead.

On the day of ordination I was happy, more happy than I could show at the time. I was also anxious. I had previously spent years and years in the company of Anglican and Roman Catholic women debating the wisdom of our joining a 'men's club' and getting caught into existing institutional norms of behaviour. Would we be swamped, coerced into acting according to male tradition rather than according to our female nature? Would we become 'clericalized' and dominate the laity in authoritarian ways? Would we be able to complement male styles of authority in new and different ways? How would the image of priesthood be changed by the inclusion of women in its ranks?

Now, five years on, I am still asking these questions. A few of my women friends seem to think that the struggle is over, 'we should just get on with the job and wait to be assimilated into the structures'. Some, however, still feel that they cannot truly be themselves, or be valued as they deserve, within a predominantly male institution where there are no women bishops. Others, having worked in the prevalent culture of male ministry, are disillusioned and are seriously considering leaving an organization which still oppresses women, denies them effective voices in the government of the Church, misuses their talents and makes no adequate provision for their childbearing and rearing roles in families.

Nevertheless, I am happy to be a priest who is a woman. I continue to try to understand how and what my womanhood contributes to my own parish ministry. I am, however, deeply saddened by the apparent loss of the precious solidarity I had with other women – and some men – during the years of struggle and waiting.

I came into the priesthood hoping for, and expecting, change. I hoped that the coming of women would end the male clergy's preoccupation with justifying their existence by overwork and multiplication of committees and structures. So far, I have seen no essential change in male attitudes towards ministry; moreover, some of the women who are now priests have assimilated an attitude of justification by works. I thought that women's delight in worshipping God in and through prayer of various kinds would change our public acts of worship – without loss of their essential form. I think this has happened to a limited extent but sometimes against fierce resistance. I expected a greater appreciation of lay talents and gifts, as well as of clergy gifts; I know that many people in the Church are working towards this end. Nevertheless, those who make decisions about ministry still seem to tolerate many situations in which lay people and clergy, stipendiary and self supporting, are being 'burnt out' by overwork, underuse of the talents of women priests and the laity and inadequate consideration for their human needs.

I believe that women priests will contribute to the fulfilment of my hopes through effecting these and other positive changes in church structure and life. Personally, I want to spend my remaining years encouraging younger women priests, and others whom

I admire and cherish, to celebrate the advent of women into the ranks of the ordained clergy and to make the fullest possible use of their gifts. Before that can happen, however, there need to be widespread changes in attitudes towards women priests whose talents and ways of working are often seen as threatening. There needs to be much more opportunity in all churches for listening to women's points of view. Nothing much will change in England and Wales until we admit women into the episcopate and wholeheartedly begin to celebrate the equal and complementary nature of men and women in the Church and society.

For myself, becoming a priest has been like coming home; for the first time in my life, I know myself to be the person who God created me to be. Priesthood has enlarged my love of my own womanhood, enabled me to appreciate and celebrate the God-given differences between men and women and, above all, to feel responsible to God for the gifts God has given me and which now can be used in a way that was formerly unknown to me. I thank God for all that.

*　　*　　*

Una Kroll felt called to priestly ministry when she was 19 years old. She spent a long period as a medical doctor, missionary, deaconess, deacon, Christian feminist, author and broadcaster, before becoming a priest when she was 71 years old. Most of her life's work has related to the plight of disadvantaged women in her own and other countries and she believes that her spiritual life has been enhanced by her work for women in society. She now lives a life of prayer as a solitary in life vows in the border town of Monmouth in Wales.

Following the Call

BLANCHE CLANCEY

My call to ministry came, suddenly, unexpectedly and unmistakably. I was sitting in an ordinary evening service; the Old Testament reading was Isaiah 6:

And I heard the voice of the Lord saying, 'Whom shall I send and who shall go for us?' Then I said 'Here am I, send me.'

In a flash it wasn't just words, I was drawn into the story, involved. At that moment I knew that I too must say, 'Here am I.' In some inexplicable way, I also knew saying this meant I was to be used in the ministry of the Church.

This all happened in 1943 when I was a schoolgirl of 14, and girls just couldn't aspire to such a calling. Some people I spoke to about my experience seemed to think it funny and laughed, others took it more seriously, but just assumed that I should become a missionary.

At that time I was a fairly biddable girl and took this advice. On leaving school I trained as a nurse in order to have an 'acceptable' feminine qualification to offer for work in the mission field. However, during my training I met the man who was later to become my husband. We married, started a family and even though we were very happy, there were times when I suffered from feelings of guilt that I had not followed the call to be a missionary.

With two pre-school children, God spoke to me again, and I realized that I was still to be used in ministry. A year or so later I became the first non-resident student at Gilmore House. I was made so welcome there and every possible effort was made to fit my lectures and practical placements with my family life.

I left there in 1967 only to find that there was no parish in my home area willing to employ a woman parish worker (the title given us at that time). So I taught RE one day each week and worked as diocesan social worker on the other days.

Then a new vicar arrived in my home parish and started to use me, both in worship and also in pastoral matters: this encouraged me to explore the possibility of becoming a deaconess. After a further selection conference, in 1978 this is what happened. A year later, when our curate was due to leave, I was invited to take his place. At first I felt elated. It seemed as if, 35 years after my girlhood experience, my call was finally going to be acknowledged.

During the time I was at Gilmore the conviction that my call was to priesthood grew more and more real. It wasn't long before the limitations placed upon me as a deaconess became, at first irksome, and then more and more deeply painful.

The next landmark for me was being appointed as deaconess in charge of two churches within a team ministry. This again promised fresh opportunities and freedom in ministry. The fact that the team rector or one of the team vicars had to come to each of my churches every Sunday to say part of the Eucharist became harder and harder. The only thing that made it bearable was the fact that they were all very much with me. One of them spoke of his feelings; he found it almost as hard as I did and had a real sense of intruding – especially in the service of holy matrimony.

During my years there I was ordained as deacon – this I found to be a very painful experience. When I was made deaconess, the bishop had said exactly the same words over me as to the men. So, perhaps in naivety, I had always hoped and prayed that the next time I was presented to a bishop it would be when I was ordained as priest. The only real difference this made to my everyday life was that I could now marry the couples I spent time with in preparation.

In 1989, having reached the age of 60, I retired and felt utterly devastated that I had waited so long and had still not seen the Church of England accept women priests. I had been in the public gallery at Church House in 1978 for the debate and left there with tears streaming down my face to walk blindly to Victoria station. Time and again I cried out to God, 'Why does it have to take so long?' I resolved to leave the Church of England at this point, but somehow, after a while, very unwillingly, I felt myself almost propelled to the local church. Gradually I began to be drawn into church life and ministry and also became very involved with MOW within the diocese. It was as representative of Southwell MOW that I was invited to be in the studio of Radio Nottingham on 11 November 1992. I agreed to go, and only when I was standing with my husband in front of the TV screens waiting for the final count did I realize that I would have to turn and run away if the vote went the wrong way. Praise God it didn't, and I was able to give something approaching a coherent live interview for the evening news slot as well as record something for the next Sunday morning programme. We then shared champagne with other deacons in the diocese and eventually went home to a manic telephone answering machine.

The interview with our bishop (theoretically a supporter) two days later had to be experienced to be believed. We were told very strictly not to show any sign of triumphalism or even joy. We all left feeling completely deflated. Eventually the ordination services took place: I managed to get a ticket to Bristol and drove home to Nottingham singing the Nunc Dimittis! When my own turn came I could hardly believe that it was happening, I can't remember any occasion in my life when I felt so fulfilled – unless it was when I presided the next Sunday at the Eucharist.

I still have a very full ministry and wait now to see the Act of Synod rescinded and women bishops – then I'll sing the Nunc Dimittis again.

*   *   *

Blanche Clancey went to a church school in south east London and developed a great appreciation of the church year and worship. She married Brian in 1953 and they had a daughter and son. Her husband and both children have been present at all her 'milestones' – Rochester Cathedral when she was ordained deaconess, Lichfield when she was made deacon and Southwell where she was priested.

Blanche adds: 'Joy was soon swamped by the news that Brian had cancer. He lived for almost two more years and even in his illness rejoiced that my calling had been fulfilled. One of the most moving things I have ever done was to sign him with ashes on Ash Wednesday.'

A Step Ahead: Church Trailing Calling

JUDITH ROSE

It was way back in 1963 when I first believed God was calling me into Christian ministry. As a farmer my first thoughts were about agricultural missionary work. It was with some initial disappointment that I discovered that God's call was to ministry in the Church of England. This was long before women could be ordained. The only avenue to full-time service was that of a parish lay worker. It was not a very exciting prospect! However, it was the conviction that this was God's calling that encouraged me to go forward and that has sustained me through some of the more difficult times. I have never regretted that decision. I thoroughly enjoyed studying theology, and found it fulfilling and a great privilege to become a Christian minister, even though in those early days I had a very limited liturgical or preaching role. My official status lay somewhere below that of a curate, but as the years went by I gained experience and was able to develop my gifts. I was very fortunate to work with some able clergy and lay people.

Frustration began to set in after I had been in the curate role for about 12 years. I still enjoyed Christian ministry and took full advantage of all the opportunities that came my way. Because it was not possible for women like myself to be ordained, the opportunity to become an incumbent was not open to us. It was during this time that I struggled with a Christian attitude to ambition. Some said that women who were seeking ordination were only looking for status. Strangely, that was never said of the men. These voices made me examine my own motives. After much thought, discussion, Bible study and prayer, I came to the conclusion that ambition is only wrong if it is selfish and at the expense of others. I genuinely wanted to offer my gifts and experience to the Church in a way that would be challenging and stimulating to others as well as myself. I spent two difficult years at the end of the 1970s searching for my next sphere of ministry. I even considered joining the Methodist Church, which had women ministers. However, my reason for becoming a Methodist did not seem good enough, and there was a sense that God was not releasing me from his call to ministry in the Church of England.

I then became chaplain at Bradford Cathedral, exercising the role of vicar to the regular congregation. This gave me increased responsibility, and again I worked with some wonderful people. In many ways those were good years. The biggest problem then was that I had responsibility without authority. I was not part of the cathedral chapter where policy decisions were taken. Sometimes those decisions undermined or ignored what I was seeking to do as pastor to the congregation. I was in effect exercising the role of an ordained priest while still being a deaconess, i.e. a lay person. With goodwill a great deal was achieved, but this was in spite of the structures.

When I needed to move, there was still the difficulty of exercising a developing ministry without the basic qualification of ordination: God's calling led me to Rochester diocese where I did the job of a team vicar on a large housing estate. Of course, I could not be a proper team vicar because I was not ordained. I met the demands for a sacramental ministry with some difficulty and only with the goodwill of fellow ordained members of the team. It was like trying to do a good job with one hand tied behind your back. However, the opportunities outweighed the limitations, and I counted myself fortunate.

At this time, I was unaware of some deep anger within me. I remember showing some lack of tolerance towards clergymen who, for whatever reason, were inadequate. On more than one occasion I helped a sick or elderly ordained man who took the priestly part of the communion service, but I had to stay alert in case he collapsed. To be male was more important than being competent, bearing in mind that both of us were called as ministers of the gospel. It was not until I was ordained priest that I realized the level of suppressed anger that had been building up over the years. To be a priest was a relief, a coming home, a recognition of what I had been in my heart for many years.

For much of my ministry it seems that I have been ahead of what the Church has allowed. I was exercising a diaconal ministry for many years before I became a deacon. Indeed, I found being made a deacon in 1987 quite a humiliating experience. The Church was rejoicing in this significant development, but I was being accepted as one of the junior clergy after having been in post for 21 years. Then, as a deacon, I was made rural dean while the lawyers debated whether it was valid for someone who was not a priest to hold this office. In 1995, I was appointed as an acting archdeacon. I was 'acting' because we awaited a minor change in church law. A few months later I was legal and became the first woman to be an archdeacon in the Church of England.

I thank God for wonderful opportunities to serve him in these ways for the past 36 years, during which there have been great changes in the role of women in the Church of England. At times, it has been difficult to reconcile God's calling with the attitude of the Church but, as in so many ways, God is often way out in front. Where the Holy Spirit leads we are called to follow. This is as true for the Church as for individuals like myself, but we need to thank God for his patience, graciousness and love.

*   *   *

Judith Rose was born in 1937. Her first career was in agriculture. After training for the ministry she became a parish worker in Swindon in 1966, and then a deaconess at St George's Church, Leeds, moving to Bradford Cathedral as chaplain in 1981. From 1985 she held a team vicar's post on a large housing estate in Kent. She was made a deacon in 1987 and shortly afterwards became the first woman rural dean in the Church of England. In 1990 she became chaplain to the Bishop of Rochester, was ordained priest in 1994, and took up the role of Archdeacon of Tonbridge in 1995. She retires in the summer of 2002. Judith was married to David Gwyer in 1991 and widowed in 2000. She has two step-daughters.

Pain and Privilege

RUTH WINTLE

I had no vocation to priesthood. My call was to full-time ministry in the Church, and I served as a lay-worker, deaconess and deacon, in a mixture of parochial, academic and administrative posts, over a period of 27 years. In a variety of contexts, I aimed to fulfil the primary goal of the ministerial gifts of Ephesians 4:11–12, 'to prepare God's people for works of service, so that the body of Christ may be built up'. It was people who mattered, the people who were Christ's Church, and my gifts were offered to help them to grow. God's leading drew me into posts of responsibility at national and diocesan level and, in 1992, I was elected as a member of the House of Clergy of the General Synod.

The pain grew as the Church divided on the issue of women's priesthood in the years leading up to the November Synod when that crucial vote was taken. It was not my pain: I had no problem. My personal ministry was secure and satisfying and, while I was in favour of women's ordination, I had no sense of a calling to that ministry. I felt keenly the Church's pain. My rural dean, opposed to priesthood for women, reached out to me in a generosity of love and supportive prayer, both before and after the vote, to which I responded in kind and in tears. I knew the depth of his hurt, and his position typified that of so many. The actual vote in the Synod left me torn between relief and sorrow, caught between the erupting joy of some and the numbing pain of others. In Church House there seemed no place to be quiet; no place to pray.

The following year was one in which the Church sought a resolution of its divisions, and in which I looked for God's will in my own life. I suppose, in a way, I had little choice. So much of my ministry was 'priestly' in nature. I wanted to affirm that the whole Church is called to a 'priesthood of all believers', and that there is no need to be ordained in order to be effective in that ministry. Because of my position in the diocese, the bishop suggested that I was not the best person to make that affirmation, and someone else said that, if I did not offer for priesting, the congregation of the church to which I was attached would probably carry me bodily to the cathedral and plonk me down in front of the ordaining bishop! As far as they were concerned I was a 'priest', and they were the ones who were outraged when, as deaconess and deacon, I led them in worship, but could not preside at the Eucharist. If anyone, it was the church members who 'called' me to ordination as a priest.

Later, of course, it was wonderful – a very special privilege to be part of a group of women making history in the Church, and to be allowed to serve as an ordained priest, set apart for that particular ministry. In many ways – in most ways – there has been little functional change, but I have sensed, in my ministry, a wholeness which was not there before. In the context of 'privilege', I search for a deeper understanding of what it means that an ordained priest stands for the people before God, and for God before the people. It certainly has nothing to do with importance, and I still find it hard to absolve and bless, to break the bread and to consecrate the wine, as though I had a right to be different. In terms of church order, I can accept the 'calling' to perform, on behalf of the gathered congregation, the priestly role of the people of God.

Just as I shrink from any 'division' between priest and people, and within that 'shrinking' find pain, so I am aware of the continuing pain of a divided Church. But triumphant love overcomes both fear and pain, and I am grateful for the privilege of priestly service, and am glad that I was not allowed to hold back when the opportunity for ordination was offered.

* * *

Canon Ruth Wintle taught for seven years in Jamaica (West Indies) after completing a degree in French at London University. Three years on the staff of the Inter-Varsity Fellowship led to training for ministry at St Michael's House in Oxford, combined with a theology degree at St Hugh's. Two years in an Oxford parish, and ministry among students, were followed by five years as a tutor at Cranmer Hall, Durham, and then nine years as an ACCM selection secretary. As a deaconess (from Durham days) she moved to Worcester diocese, served as Director of Ordinands, as Adviser in Women's Ministry and on the bishop's staff. Ordained deacon in 1987, appointed Honorary Canon of the cathedral the same year, she was priested in 1994, and retired in December 1997.

Journey Beyond Priesthood

JEAN MAYLAND

Thirty-eight of us were ordained on two consecutive days in Durham Cathedral in May 1994. I was ordained on Trinity Sunday, which was also the fortieth anniversary of Bishop David Jenkins' own ordination to the priesthood. To mark the occasion we gave him 40 red roses after the service and joined in the laughter and the tears. Chris Sterry, a friend with whom I had taught on the Northern Ordination Course, said that he had never been to an ordination of such 'aweful' holiness in the very best sense of the word. 'If anyone could call down the Holy Spirit,' he said, 'Bishop David could.'

When my husband turned 70, Bishop Michael Turnbull decided that he must retire from being non-stipendiary priest in Brancepeth. Bishop Michael suggested that I should give up part of my ecumenical job and have a parish of my own. This I would have loved after the long, long wait but sadly the offer had come too late. Ralph, my husband, felt he could not face being at the centre of parish life any more, even if the parish was mine. At first I was angry, feeling that I had supported him for years, and now he could not support me. Then I decided that I could not go on being angry after 36 years of marriage, and so I applied for the post of associate secretary for the Community of Women and Men in the Church, at the Council of Churches for Britain and Ireland (CCBI). When that post was devolved to the national ecumenical bodies, I succeeded the Revd Dr Colin Davey as co-ordinating secretary for church life at the renamed Churches Together in Britain and Ireland (CTBI).

From a pastoral point of view I am sad that I have never had care of a parish of my own. It is made all the more difficult in that I have never been used or recognized as an NSM priest in the diocese of York, where my home is, as Colin was recognized and used in his home diocese of St Albans. The rural dean is 'Forward in Faith' and the priest in charge of the four villages of which ours is one, did not want anyone to help in his patch. He only had one service a Sunday for the four villages and expected people to travel around. Naturally the congregations declined and the churches began to die. When he retired they were told the diocese could not afford another priest for them and they were joined with a seaside town parish six miles away.

At Easter 2002 the new woman parish priest decreed that there would not be an Easter communion in any of the four village churches. All must travel to her parish church in the seaside town. The reason given is that she must establish her authority and build up relations. All offers of help by my husband and myself have been rejected. We are both used to working in a team and notice with concern that the majority of clergy in the Church of England are jealous of their authority and position and seem incapable of working with others for the sake of the gospel. It makes me particularly sad when women behave in this way. To my mind, it is absolutely no good women being ordained priest unless we are willing to try to remodel the Church and change the priesthood. Both Church and priesthood need a circular and co-operative model, instead of a pyramid, hierarchical one. I know it is hard for women in parishes as they do constantly have to prove themselves, but we must not be forced into letting go of our vision.

One of the joys of my job is that I can keep the vision and work towards it. I can also practise a little gentle boat-rocking on behalf of my Roman Catholic and Orthodox brothers and sisters. I was able to share with the Roman Catholic Women at the first international conference of Women's Ordination World Wide (WOW) in Dublin in 2001. I also attended a conference at an Orthodox Monastery in Athens and was asked to speak publicly about my vocation as a priest. Afterwards Colin Davey told me that it was the monastery where he and the other members of the Anglican Orthodox Conversations had been anathematized when the Church of England began seriously to consider the ordination of women to the priesthood. Times do change!

In turn I have been upheld and strengthened by my URC and Methodist friends. When the URC refuse even to consider for their ministry any man who will not fully accept women's ministry, I pray one day the Church of England may do the same. When Dr John Taylor says at the press conference launching the report of the Anglican Methodist Conversations that the opening of all ministries for women is for the Methodists 'non negotiable', I thank God for their witness.

I find my priesthood is recognized by other churches, and I have had the joy and privilege of presiding at communion in Methodist and United Reformed Churches. Within the Church of England I owe a great deal to the vicar of St John's, Waterloo, who invites me to preside at lunch-hour Eucharists. When I moved my London base to Grays in Essex, the vicar, who is also the rural dean, immediately made me welcome and invited me to take services during interregna in his deanery whenever I had Saturday meetings in London, and was not going home for the weekend. It helps to heal some of the pain I feel when I go to my own home at weekends and find my priesthood rejected by fellow clergy, although not by the people. Even there the Methodists welcome me to take services. It is this strange mixture of loving the Church of England with every fibre of my being and yet so often being rejected by it, and of being helped and healed and valued by people of other churches. Not quite what I expected when I was ordained priest in Durham Cathedral – but then our God is a God of surprises!

* * *

Jean Mayland was born in Stoke-on-Trent and educated at the Orme Girls' School, Newcastle under Lyme, and Lady Margaret Hall, Oxford, where she read history and then theology. She taught in a number of schools and colleges and on both the Northern and the North Eastern Ordination Course. Jean was a lay member of Church Assembly and General Synod for 25 years and an active magistrate for over 20 years. She served on the Liturgical Commission and on the Central Committee of the World Council of Churches. She was the Moderator of the Study Commission of the Conference of European Churches. Jean was ordained deacon in 1991 and priest in 1994.

Still Far to Go

DONALD BARNES

In the heady aftermath of 11 November 1992 one thing impressed me more than any other. Not the cheering and singing outside Church House, but the way in which many ordinary people, many of whom had not darkened a church for years, would stop me in the street and tell me how pleased they were. The Church had done something which the Decade of Evangelism had singularly failed to do. It had caught the public imagination. They felt caught up in what had happened. Like Berlin and South Africa, another wall had fallen!

It was sad that the bishops did not sense this national mood. 'Women to be priests', sang the media. 'Don't cheer please! We are Anglicans', was the official reply. Not an exceptional opportunity but a case for damage limitation. So we moved into the area of 'the London Plan', 'the Act of Synod', 'the Two Integrities' and 'the Flying Bishops'. Instead of helping to heal those devastated by the vote, they were allowed to pretend that it had not happened or at least was not for real.

However, nothing could take away the explosion of joy at these first ordinations. Penny Jamieson, Bishop of Dunedin in New Zealand, came literally from the end of the earth to preach at the Service of Thanksgiving in Ripon Cathedral. Forbidden by the Archbishop of York to wear a mitre, she was supported by all the other visiting bishops who likewise abstained.

Our ordinations in the London diocese were especially poignant. Five of the six bishops, including Richard Chartres, refused to participate. Our own parish deacon was ordained in the cathedral by the redoubtable Roy Williamson, Bishop of Southwark, who made no secret of his great happiness to officiate. Next day in high celebration, Claire, our new priest, presided at the Eucharist with other parishes joining Lis. For me this was the fulfilment of many years' service with women in ministry.

Deaconess Win Hambly had been with me for 19 years. Her patient and loving work convinced me that gender could be no bar to priesthood. In the days when the Edmonton Episcopal Area was a much more open and inclusive place, Deaconess Gill Cooke was appointed to be effectively in charge of our Conventional District. I was delighted in 1994 to assist in her ordination in York Minster and to preach at her first eucharistic celebration in Hull prison where she was assistant chaplain.

Claire Wilson came to our parish as a deacon in 1987. She was well-known in the locality and had been a very successful teacher in a comprehensive school. German was one of her subjects, and I remember a joint interview which we gave to German television before the vote – her contribution needed no translation! She is a very able preacher and widely read in theology, has excellent pastoral gifts and is a good organizer. I found her a stimulating colleague who did not duck awkward questions. She kept up a lively dialogue, especially with the male clergy.

As my retirement was close, a number of people felt that she would be a popular successor, and although our bishop was opposed, the patrons, Westminster Abbey, had given strong support to the cause. Claire herself was cautious. She decided to apply and remained on during the interregnum, but in the end was not appointed. I was sorry for her and for the number of people in the parish who were very disappointed. Local feeling was strong, but the patrons were unmoved. I felt that a great opportunity had been missed, not least because our parish would have been the first in the Edmonton Episcopal Area to have had a woman as incumbent. (Eight years later there is still no woman in that position.) It would have been a tremendous boost to the general morale of the women there.

Claire joined the list of Edmonton exiles. She is now happily settled in the Chelmsford diocese. I think of others – Elaine, after a difficult time moved to Stepney, where she became area dean; Joanna, after running an important parish with great success during an interregnum, reluctantly left London for a prestigious job in Leeds; Ruth, ordained separately from her male colleagues, returned quickly to Cambridge; Marjorie, sent off, like most women candidates, to another area.

What a waste of talented people and what a deprivation for members of ordinary laity – men as well as women – who would be delighted to enjoy their ministry but are denied the opportunity. We have come a long way, but we need effective leaders who will make no secret of how much they value and affirm half of the human race in the ministry of the Church.

*   *   *

Donald Barnes was born in 1926 and educated at Westcliffe High School, Kings College, London and Warminster. He was ordained in 1952 in London Diocese, and served as assistant curate at St Matthew, Willesden, and was vicar of St Peter, Cricklewood, for 20 years (assisted by Deaconess W.K. Hambly). As vicar of St Peter, Belsize Park, he was assisted by Revd Claire Wilson. He was area dean of North Camden (1983–88), and served on General Synod (1985–95), and was area warden of readers (1980–95). He was also a lecturer at Bishop College, Cheshunt, and taught on the North Thames Ordination Course. He was an industrial chaplain at United Biscuits, Harlesden, and a member of MOW, WATCH, MCU and GRAS. He is married to Sally and has three children and five grandchildren.

Spiritual Sign and Good Stewardship

JOHN DAVIES

I voted for the ordination of women to the priesthood for two main reasons.

One was my belief that the Church should be a sign of the inclusive justice of God. In South Africa, where I served as a priest for 15 years, the Church was called to struggle against a demonic type of discrimination; we were inspired by the traditional doctrine of the Church as the visible body of Christ. So, to me, it was no surprise that the Anglican Church in South Africa, because of – not in spite of – its strong Catholic tradition, saw the movement towards the ordination of women as part of the struggle against discrimination. It decided to act accordingly, with relative ease.

Second, there was a very practical motive. In Shrewsbury, for which I had responsibility as bishop, I felt that we were not making the best possible use of the human resources with which we had been entrusted. For some years, we had been following the example of our neighbours in Wales, by licensing some experienced women deacons as resident ministers; this meant that in effect they were ministers-in-charge of parishes. They were licensed as local leaders in mission and ministry. They were chairing their Parochial Church Councils. But as deacons, their leadership was not integrated with a ministry of Eucharist and absolution. This deployment of women deacons was fruitful and good; but it was seriously incomplete.

So, one of the most significant features of these ordinations in 1994 was not just that we were ordaining female people but that we were ordaining exceptionally experienced people. Normally, Anglican ministers are ordained to the priesthood after only one year as deacons, and we gradually move into leadership positions over a period of several subsequent years. Priesthood, leadership and ministerial authority are a bundle of commitments which

most ministers gradually take up without separating out the
different elements. But, many of our candidates for priesting in
the spring of 1994 had been deacons for several years; some had
been deaconesses for even longer; and some, as I have said, had
been chairing PCCs. In most ways, these had been 'vicars', and
had been recognized as such. But they had not been priests. They
had not had the very visible and public authority to preside at the
Eucharist; nor had they had the much less visible, but equally
significant, authority to act as ministers of the sacrament of
reconciliation. This, then, has been a unique opportunity to
observe and identify the specific differences which priestly
ordination can make, both for the minister and for the rest of the
disciple-community.

All this contributed to a widely positive attitude to this ordination, as we experienced it in Shropshire. Like other areas, we
had careful and thorough consultations, in which the lay people
of the parishes were properly represented. Rural communities
are often said to be 'conservative'. If this is true, it is the conser-
vatism of people who want to look carefully at practicalities and
who are sceptical about more abstract theories. Time and again,
lay people from the rural parishes were insisting that what they
wanted were good and caring pastors. This came out vividly at a
consultation at Wem. I had rather expected that there might be
quite a lot of opposition to the ordination of women at this meeting. The parish of Myddte had a previous commitment and was
unable to send representatives. This was a parish where we had
licensed a senior woman deacon as resident minister. They sent a
letter to the meeting, saying something like this:

> We were a bit dubious at first about having a woman as our
> minister. But we can tell you, don't worry. We have never
> before had such good pastoral care and leadership as we are
> now getting from our 'Vicar'. If they are all like her, the future
> is going to be very bright for us all. Go for it!

Personal friendships counted for a great deal. One of our
clergy had been a vigorous opponent; but, when the date of the
priesting of his female colleague was announced, he insisted that
nothing was going stop him from sharing in her ordination.
Another priest, who had similar theological opinions, generously

provided facilities in his church for a women deacon who was a minister with specialist responsibilities. As we said to each other, 'with opponents like this, who needs friends?'

There were, of course, some less happy experiences. But, with due care, I was able to say that I reckoned that there was no need for the ministry of Provincial Episcopal Visitors in our area. This was not because we all agreed. But both clergy and lay people are used to being led by bishops with whom they do not agree in every particular. They would prefer the ministry of a bishop with whom they disagree but who belongs in their area and shares their horizons, rather than have a stranger sent in for special occasions. For the clergy, especially, this represents something close to the heart of the gospel, and it is one of the main lessons, for me, of the whole process. We are given to each other. We 'accept each other as Christ has accepted us'. Our being-in-communion with each other does not depend on our agreeing with each other or approving of each other. Our being-in-communion is the gift of Christ. In an episcopal church, this is translated into practice by the fact that clergy are called and put into fellowship with each other by the bishop's act of licensing. Within a deanery chapter, for instance, we do not choose who is in the team with us. We accept each other, as part of our obedience to the bishop. This means that our normal fellowship together can be a sign of the gospel. I reckon that this has been demonstrated in practice by the way that, on the whole, women and men have accepted each other as priests.

*   *   *

John Davies was area bishop of Shrewsbury in the diocese of Lichfield from 1987 to 1994. Previously he had been a parish priest and university chaplain in South Africa, Wales and England.

From Theological Assent to Cultural Normality: A Slow Progress

VINCENT STRUDWICK

The formative years when my vocation was stirred, recognized and nurtured were the 1940s and 50s, in smoke-filled churches and smoke-filled studies where the incense from Prinknash and the pipe smoke from 'Three Nuns' tobacco mingled in comfortable aromas that can still recall and rekindle the experience.

Both the measured, dignified male-dominated worship, and the theological learning of my pipe-smoking 'fathers' seemed at the time the natural cultural clothing for the gospel as I had received it. It was the 'culture' of the Church into which I had been born and was coming to love. I wanted to be part of it as I tried to interpret and respond to God's call.

I think the first time I felt a pang of nervousness and doubt about this culture was years after in the 1960s when I was a priest and a member of a religious community. I went to celebrate the Eucharist for some nuns in a nearby convent. Following the service, I was led to a full English breakfast in the 'parlour' while the nuns nibbled a crust in the nearby refectory. As I reached for the knife and fork I realized that each was engraved with the word 'priest'; presumably so that no lay female lips might contaminate them.

This left me uneasy and was (as far as I can remember) the beginning of a growing realization about gender issues and the role of women in the Church's ministry, which became increasingly important for me. I can remember initiating girl servers at the altar of our guest house chapel, which seemed to make some of my brethren regard me as a sexual deviant; but it was with the help and encouragement of others of those 'old fathers' who had influenced me, and by studying both early church history and the development of the Church of England, that my interest developed into a positive desire to see women ordained as priests, as part of a radical reshaping of the Church's life and its future engagement in mission in a changing society.

During the 1980s I became aware of the way in which the issue of the ordination of women was shattering the unity of the Episcopal Church in the United States, and as American friends of 20 years and more became 'distant' when they realized where I stood, I became more and more convinced that this was not a single issue, but part of a larger canvas involving the reshaping of the Christian Church in a new culture.

It is, however, one thing to embrace an idea, to speak for it – even to work for it, as I did from 1988 as principal of a non-residential course training men and women for ordination. It is another to be transformed by it. I later realized that my education was only just beginning, for what has to happen is that theological principle and spiritual insight have to be reclothed in new patterns of belonging and living – a cultural transformation.

The vice-principal of the course was a woman who became first deacon, then priest, while other members of the staff were male. Although liturgically and in the academic and pastoral disciplines of the programme I think we modelled a 'team', what the vice-principal experienced was an underlying 'boys' club' culture that undermined both her belonging and her participation in her role. Of course, I couldn't see it! It wasn't that we were not courteous, correct and well-intentioned. It was as if (and I can only speak for myself) that 'normal' was what I had grown up with, and what was being experienced was good, necessary and godly – but not 'normal'. For it to become normal, I had to go through a process of 'losing' the old before I could thoroughly participate in the new. During the early Elizabethan age it was reported that parts of London looked like a battle ground, as desecrated and demolished monasteries stood as witness to what had been, before the rebuilding of new structures of spiritual and corporate life could begin. In my experience, the Church of England has changed. Some things that were part of it, and normal, are now gone.

Over the years my education has continued, as it has since semi-retirement, when I am still able to assist a women priest in a non-parochial cure. Now I not only know it is 'normal' but it feels 'normal', as it has become for thousands of parishioners who have experienced having a woman rector, or vicar or curate.

I believe, however, that the breakthrough in mission to which I look forward will not come until this feeling of normality is experienced throughout the institutional life of the Church of England, from bottom to top. It will only come when ordained women are exercising their priesthood and episcopal ministry in all areas of the Church's life. When this is so, and the theological judgements and pastoral insights that have led to change are transforming the Church's life, then there is some chance that our Church will be renewed.

The Church of England has new things to learn, not dreamed of by my friends and mentors of a past age who nurtured me into the Church of England as it then was. But that was another country, so to speak; another world. As I listen to the stories of my friends who are women priests I realize both how far we have come, but also how far we have to travel for the radical reshaping that we need in order to be the Church in today's – let alone tomorrow's – world.

*   *   *

Vincent Strudwick is chamberlain and emeritus fellow of Kellogg College in the University of Oxford. After service in the RAF he trained at Kelham where from 1956 he was a member of the Society of the Sacred Mission. From 1960–70 he was sub-warden and lecturer in church history at the theological college at Kelham, from where he also gained experience in Southern Africa and the United States. After leaving the community he held a variety of educational and teaching appointments from Sussex through Milton Keynes to Oxford. He became a canon of Christ Church, Oxford, in 1981.

Moving Towards Wholeness

PATIENCE PURCHAS

'Blessing' is the word that comes to my mind when I think about the ordination of women. Years ago, when we were debating the issue in Diocesan Synod, I quoted some words from Cowper's hymn 'God moves in a mysterious way': 'Ye fearful saints, fresh courage take,/ The clouds ye so much dread/ Are big with mercy, and shall break/ In blessings on your head.' Because some tried to alarm people with a dreadful prospect were women to be ordained priest, it seemed to me important to say that what was being offered to the Church was a blessing, not a curse. I have recently been able to give evidence at two meetings where the theological issues surrounding women bishops were being discussed. Most of the discussion covered old, familiar ground and, heaven knows, that was well-trodden in the years leading up to the decision to admit women to the priesthood. My contribution was simple and supported with clear evidence. We have experienced the ministry of women priests for some eight years and their ministry is widely recognized as having been a great blessing to the Church. Indeed, I believe that when the history of the Church of England in the late twentieth and early twenty-first centuries comes to be written, the introduction of women into the priesthood will be recorded as a one of our great successes.

My particular journey in ministry has coincided with the movement towards the ordination of women. Much as I tried to avoid making it a personal campaign to further my own interests, I have to say that as I followed the issues, so my own vocation grew. I trained for the ministry in the late 1970s when the national debate was hotting up and I became an active member of MOW, first at diocesan and then at national level. After ten years in ministry, I was elected to General Synod by the clergy of St Albans diocese and I was there to vote on 11 November 1992. Soon after, I was appointed to a post in the diocese as Assistant

(now Associate) Diocesan Director of Ordinands which included
responsibility for women's ministry. Since then, I have had a
fairly high profile within the Church of England and have taken
a particular delight in observing and encouraging the developing
ministry of women. I have seen women appointed as incumbents
of parishes which have been run down or even severely neglected
and love them into life and growth. I have seen women who have
served long years as assistants in parishes blossoming as, at last,
they were given appropriate responsibility. In my work as DDO,
I meet women of all ages, some of great ability and spiritual
insight, and I watch their developing ministries with a pride that
is, I admit, sometimes rather maternal.

The new generation of women priests have still to contend
with the opposition of a diminishing minority within the Church,
but they forge ahead. Quite rightly, they do not want to be
fettered by the inhibitions of an older generation. We had to
tread carefully and cautiously and not expect too much, too
soon. Some of us carry scars to this day. I am aware of a raw
nerve or two which can still make me jump, though I have been
saved from the more painful encounters with the opposition.

I am married to a priest and this has given me a privileged position to some extent, as has my post as a senior member of the
bishop's staff. In any case, St Albans diocese does not have a
large number of people opposed to women priests. I have had a
few experiences of people indicating that they disapprove of
women priests when I have gone to take a service as a visiting
celebrant or administered communion at cathedral services. But
these can be set against so many affirming experiences that the
negative ones seem of small account. Nationally, I have worked
to build friendships with some of those opposed and have always
operated within the conscience provision the Synod agreed to,
though that has not always protected me from the spite and
anger of the disaffected. Some have a harder time and suffer
within a system that is essentially discriminatory. I am proud of
the women priests of the Church of England, not least because of
the generous and forbearing way in which they have dealt with
those who cannot, or will not, recognize their ministry.

Years ago, when I was a deaconess, there was a service in
Westminster Abbey to honour the Revd Li Tim Oi, the first
woman to be ordained in the Anglican communion. The proces-

sion of robed ministers into the Abbey was arranged in such a way that the priests and deacons – all male except for a sprinkling of Americans – took their places at the front of the congregation. As the long line of blue robed deaconesses followed in, we found that there was a place waiting for us by each man. It was a marvellous prophetic sign of what an inclusive priesthood could mean. That sign sustained me through some dark hours and still inspires me. It is that cheering image of men and women working side by side in the Lord's service that I care about, a model of wholeness in a broken world.

I am not fearful for the future nor am I fussed by the threats and dire warnings of those who dream that the decision to ordain women can be reversed. The language of 'discernment and reception' becomes more irrelevant with each day that passes. There will be no going back, rather I am confident that the women priests of the Church of England will go from strength to strength. The women of my generation are near retirement. We shall not be the group from which the first women bishops are chosen, but ours has been the joy of leading the way into the priesthood. It has been a special blessing. Thanks be to God.

*   *   *

Patience Purchas has belonged to the Church of England since her teens. Married to a priest for 33 years and the mother of two married daughters, she was made a deaconess in 1980 and worked in local radio. After her ordination as a deacon in 1987 she worked as an NSM in her parish and in varous diocesan tasks and then, shortly before her priesting, as Assistant (now Associate) Director of Ordinands for St Albans diocese. She is a member of the Bishop of St Albans Senior Staff and an honorary canon. She has been a member of General Synod since 1990 and has served on a number of committees and working parties, including that set up to review the way bishops are appointed.

The Highs and Lows of Being First

CHRISTINE FARRINGTON

Looking back, the last ten years have been a roller-coaster ride of highs and lows of emotion and experiences. Voting in the General Synod on that momentous November day, I could not have begun to imagine the joys that the journey of priesthood would bring, nor the occasional depths of despair to which I have been reduced.

It has been hard being the 'first woman' in so many situations: with male colleagues at Salisbury Cathedral, among the honorary canons at Ely, in my present parish. Being 'first' means being on one's own, without an immediate peer group, which can sometimes seem a lonely place to be. I feel much less new now, of course, but still on occasion when I relax into being 'one of the boys' I can get taken by surprise and angered at the feeling that yet again, I have gone invisible, and others apparently deaf. With the loveliest of male colleagues, and I really have been blessed with almost all of mine, there can be a real frustration at their wish to work with their heads, when I am engaged with my feelings, and their collective sensitivity is stretched to its limits to understand why I seem to be tetchy at the apparent lack of our communication. However, the arrival of an Easter card from my suffragan bishop this year gave me great hope: it was a cartoon by Riana Duncan of five men and one woman sitting round a table, engaged in a meeting. The chairman is saying, 'That's an excellent suggestion, Miss Triggs. Perhaps one of the men here would like to make it.' I think that years on, the penny *is* beginning to drop, at least for some of the men.

I look back on chapters of priestly ministry which have been so privileged, and most of the time, such fun, although paradoxically, it has been harder at times to keep God at the centre than I would have thought. I have had opportunities of preaching and leading worship in cathedrals and tiny medieval village churches, of an annual preachment at the Chapel Royal at St James' Palace, as one of Her Majesty's chaplains, and of officiating on the 100th anniversary of a great uncle's winning the Victoria Cross. This included a rededication of his grave, with full military honours and a reception at the Tower of London where he had been a Yeoman of the Guard.

I have been through cassocks of four different colours: deaconess blue, Salisbury green, priestly black and now royal red. I enjoy being a scarlet woman, by royal appointment! Each year now until I am 70, I will attend, on duty, a Buckingham Palace garden party. In my red cassock I have got used to curious comments ('Excuse me, but what does your red dress mean you are?'); to requests for help ('Where are the gents' loos, please?'); and to semi-abusive remarks ('Do you know you're the only woman here who's forgotten to wear a hat?'). I now know the best vantage-points for celebrity-spotting, and for judging when it is best to go to the tea tent.

My happiest memories are of pastoral encounters: of putting together a service for a couple whose marriage was on the rocks, but is just now starting to mend, and who want God's blessing as they come publicly to renew their marriage vows. There is the memory of a family of five teenagers, now orphaned following the death from cancer of their mother, who wanted to dispense with undertakers, and do absolutely everything themselves to put together a funeral service they considered fitting for their mother. It included making the coffin, digging the grave, acting as pall-bearers and each of the young people contributing something to the service in church. The result was probably the most moving and meaningful service over which I've ever 'presided'. Being pastor to ordinands, to academics, to dear elderly ladies, to a young man with learning difficulties, to bouncy young confirmation candidates, to undergraduates and college fellows, to the 100 or so people who it has been my privilege as Diocesan Director of Ordinands to see through selection conferences – all these people have brought such richness to my own life and spiritual growth: it has been an enormous privilege to have been involved with them.

I cannot help comparing the journey through the diaconate to priesthood of the women ordinands I now deal with, with the slow and tortuous waiting that many of us 'oldies' had to face. I rejoice with them at their matter-of-factness at the normality of their ministry, and at the same time I rejoice at the experience of waiting that was ours. It is so special, week by week, to preside at our parish communion service, and to know my priesthood owned and made real by the congregation I serve. In a parish where *all* the ordained staff are women, I now have to assure some of the little boys that it really is possible for them to grow up to be priests as well!

*   *   *

Following a fulfilling career in the probation service, as practioner, trainer and administrator, Christine was made deaconess in the St Albans diocese in 1982, and was elected to the General Synod in 1985. She moved to Lincoln in 1986, as assistant prison chaplain and pastoral studies tutor at the theological college. Ordained deacon in 1987 she became cathedral deacon at Salisbury, where she directed a new ecumenical study centre. In 1993 she was appointed co-diocesan Director of Ordinands and Director of Women's Ministry in Ely and made an honorary canon. She was priested in 1994. Two years later she also became vicar of St Mark's, Cambridge, chaplain of Wolfson College, county chaplain of the St John Ambulance Brigade, and since 1998, chaplain to the Queen. In August 2002 she retired back to St Albans.

Healing and Integration

ANNE TOWNSEND

I learned young that preventing disturbing family discussions meant I must never raise the possibility that one day women might be ordained.

Mother quietly campaigned in the General Synod, writing to the press in her maiden name to save Father the embarrassment of his name being associated with something he was opposed to. I did what a go-ahead woman 'with a vocation' like me could do – I trained as a doctor and worked in the developing world as a medical missionary till my early 40s.

In midlife, I became founding editor of a religious family magazine, and from there was headhunted to be the national director of an evangelical charity. I accepted with reservations. At this time, few women had the opportunity of public leadership in this segment of church life. Female leaders were dangerously unscriptural creatures, who assumed 'headship' over men. They were suspect. I paid a price for being such a woman at a time when the evangelical wing of the Church was experimenting with female leadership. But it was also exhilarating.

Aged 50, I found myself thinking, 'Do it now, or you'll be too old!' The insistent gentle conviction that, of all crazy things, I was one of those called to offer themselves for ordination would not disappear. I could temporarily rationalize myself out of it – all that training, at my age, I'd earned a rest, there was no guarantee that women would ever be ordained as priests. The aching sense of calling persisted.

Finally, I told myself, 'Go for it!' Initially, I didn't tell Father (who was by then a priest) in case he talked me out of it. Well into my training, I let him into the secret. He said little. I didn't know whether he was pleased or disappointed. It was during the filming of a television documentary that he reached over, in front of the cameras, for his home communion set. Voice breaking, he presented me with the precious box, 'You can't use it yet, but one day I know you'll be allowed to.'

It hurt when those men ordained deacon with me were priested and I wasn't. I didn't want to wilt in the face of injustice and disappointment, and agreed to read the Gospel at their ordination. I risked breaking down publicly. But those men strengthened me by insisting that they would receive their first communion as priests from my hands only. Such male affirmation saw me through years of discouragement and the thought that I was crazy for taking this on.

Two years after being deaconed, the bishop appointed me as area dean for non-stipendiary ministers. This meant that I attended all meetings for rural deans. Not only was I the only person present who was not yet a priest, but also I was the only woman. At times, I felt sick with anxiety at the thought of being trapped, defenceless with such powerful men – some bitterly opposed to women being priested. My archdeacon, from a different perspective, once asked me how I felt 'being such a powerful women, who most of those men are terrified of?' Shocked, I blurted out, 'Like a scared four year old!' He had seen my adult self in action and didn't quite believe me.

People who were sexually abused as children with consequent emotional wounds and who no longer know what to make of 'God', and clergy reaching breaking-point from internal and external conflicts, were among those who found their way to my door. I quietly tried to show what a woman my age could be and achieve in the peculiarly masculine church world.

I didn't know whether anyone saw anything they desired enough to make them vote that the likes of me should be ordained priest. When the vote was positive, I wept my way home, wanting to shout out in joy to fellow Underground passengers, 'I'm going to be a priest!'

Memories of celebrating my first Eucharist move me. Mother came, but Father was too old and frail to attend. I placed his tiny home communion chalice in the centre of the altar. Tears would have streamed down my face had I not restrained them. I longed for Father's presence, rejoicing at his daughter being that which the family had struggled over for much of my life.

This was the first occasion when a female voice sang the priest's words. My soprano contrasted with the familiar tenor –

clear and complementing what had gone before. For a brief second, my heart stopped terrified: 'You're female, you can't do this!' A firm voice replied, 'Rubbish!' Briefly, when breaking the bread, a pang struck me. I felt as if I were holding a newborn grandchild and his fragile body was broken, crushed by the weight of the world. Simultaneously, I merged with all those mothers whose adult sons (human and divine) had died for others.

A good friend in my church told me that much as she loved me, she would never be reconciled to female priests. After the service she tearfully admitted, 'It was your singing that finished me . . . you'll need more stoles . . . I'll make them.'

My church thought hard about celebrating female priesthood. They knew what to do for men, but this was something different. How could they celebrate this new thing? At the end of the service they presented me with white orchids. Then the children's flute orchestra played softly, and all children (including those who could just about toddle) danced in rehearsed formations around the aisles. At a given signal, they disappeared, then suddenly stampeded forwards, heading for me, each bearing a bunch of flowers.

I was a grandmother when ordained and, perhaps, as a priest I value my grandmotherly qualities most highly. As an NSM priest, I still work full-time as a psychotherapist, exercising my priestly ministry in helping to bring about the healing integration central to both Christianity and psychotherapy.

At last, I have come into my own. Priest is what I was meant to be.

* * *

Anne Townsend was ordained deacon in 1992 and priest in 1994. Prior to that she worked with the Overseas Missionary Fellowship as a medical doctor in Thailand for 16 years. She was then editor of *Family* magazine, followed by being national director for Care Trust. She trained as a counsellor with the Richmond Fellowship and worked as a lay chaplain at St George's Hospital, London, while training on the Southwark ordination course. She trained with the Guild of Psychotherapists and was accredited by UKCP in 1999. Her books include *Faith Without Pretending* and *Good Enough for God*.

The Gift of an Altar

JANE BASS

There was one day in the distant past that marked the beginning of a long journey. It was a glorious summer day and I was on my way home from seeing my spiritual director. I was enjoying the drive, and a time of solitude without the children, when a still, quiet voice said, 'I want you to be a priest.' I was nearly paralysed with shock and pulled into the nearest coffee shop for a stiff black coffee and to consider what manner of request this was or whether I had gone dotty in the hot sun.

Through the work I had done for the Mothers' Union I had known women who openly said that they felt they had a vocation, but it was something I had never felt or aspired to. How could I? My education was varied but limited and, being left-handed and dyslexic, I had learned from the system that there was little point in trying to be academic. Yet here I was at 29, happily married with two small children, being told to do the impossible. Surely God was joking! Family and friends had in fact been telling me that I ought to be a priest, but I had dismissed the idea as folly on their part.

But it was not folly, as I slowly discovered, and as those around me continued to push me on, until St George's Day 1994 when, with many other women, I stood in St Albans Abbey, waiting for that moment of ordination. It had indeed been a long time coming. My apprenticeship had started way back in my misty youth, and continued through my becoming a deaconess in 1979, a deacon eight years later and then a priest.

Memories flood this time, but one that will always remain clear and dear, was the gift of a piece of wood.

The community church that I started in 1984 had grown and developed into a lively all-age group. They had difficulty in understanding why I was not a priest, and when I was made deacon in 1987, they insisted on calling me 'Archdeacon'. When

I was finally priested they immediately asked the suffragan bishop when I would be a bishop. There was no way of stopping their enthusiasm. As one member told me at the very first service on the site, 'Where have you been? We have waited 39 years for you.' Their pure eagerness and enthusiasm were a joy rarely seen in many Christian communities, and their expectations far outstripped the reality of our dearly beloved Church of England.

As the day of my priesting drew near a fresh problem presented itself. Where would I say my first mass? We had no altar in the community centre – it was not a customary part of the council's standard equipment. Our committee discussed the problem and concluded they would have to find a carpenter to make one. With the help of a local wood turner they decided on a portable altar top, legless, so that I could take it anywhere to use.

We were not considered to be a 'proper' church, so we did not need a faculty for this rare gift, which was just as well because the details were only settled in the weeks before my ordination. When I arrived to preside for the first time, the centre was full and the altar top in place. The service began with a blessing of the altar. That service was the fulfilment of the hopes and prayers of many years, brought joyfully together. I was surrounded by so many people who had willed this day for me, and I was aware of the love and care of a very special Christian community that had travelled with and supported me through good times and bad.

Since then I have moved on, and the folk insisted that I took my altar with me so that wherever I was it would always be there ready for use. I treasure it because it came with so much encouragement and prayer, so that even the worst moments of ministry are put into perspective when I recall the gift of my hallowed piece of wood.

After leaving the community church I moved to a long-established parish and quickly ran into the restrictions and frustrations of a 'proper church'. My first Easter as vicar told me that I had truly arrived in the Church of England. The church was stacked with white lilies and my nose was suffering from an overdose of pollen. The eight o'clock service had gone well, and we were busy wishing one another a happy Easter, when I became aware of two women conversing in worried tones about the flowers. 'It's not right,' said one. 'No, it isn't!' said the other.

Seeing nothing amiss I asked what was wrong. 'Well, you see,' they chorused, 'They go up and they should go down!' No explanation was forthcoming as I followed the 'flower ladies' up the aisle, but when we reached the chancel steps the leader screeched, 'They've pinched me lilies!' It turned out that the blooms in question had been donated individually in memory of departed loved ones but were now dispersed anonymously in other flower arrangements elsewhere in the building.

The first mass of Easter had lifted my mind and heart to the joy of the resurrection, and I had prayed that all those worshipping with me might feel the same. The flower ladies brought me down to earth with a bump, and I realized that we all had far to go, and that being a vicar meant, among other things, understanding the importance of flowers, lest I remain forever in the bad books of the Flower Guild!

*   *   *

Jane Bass, like many women priests, had a long preparation before she was ordained. An undiagnosed dyslexic, left-handed and unhappy with her education, she nevertheless survived theological college and was ordained deaconess in 1979. She has served all her ministry in parishes on the cutting-edge, planting churches and working in multifaith areas where white people have been in the minority. But her heart has always been in mission, with an emphasis on the role of catholic worship as an evangelistic tool. In addition to parish work she is International Rector of the Society of Catholic Priests – the first woman to hold this position. She is married and has two married daughters and three gorgeous grandchildren.

Being a Role Model

ROSALIND BROWN

My story is slightly different from the others, since I observed most of the first ten years from the United States where I was ordained without any battles. I moved there with no intention of being ordained, tested my vocation at the request of my community and chose an ecumenical seminary where women's ordination was assumed. Looking back, I think I took it for granted the gift of the many ordained women in the diocese and at seminary as they modelled a feminine priesthood with grace, vibrancy and delight in their vocation, although some spoke first hand of the personal cost in the early years. When news came of the vote in England, we rejoiced.

Once ordained, I was vicar of a church where, although a few people were initially uncertain because they had never had a woman before, I was welcomed with open arms. Two encounters from those years stand out as I write this. I was buying petrol when a young woman ran across the garage forecourt calling, 'Are you a priest?' The tone of her voice indicated excitement, and she insisted that I go to her car to meet her family. She was Orthodox, her husband Roman Catholic, and in her joy in discovering that women could be ordained she said, 'Having met you, I realize that I can stand before God equal with my husband.' His smile revealed delight. On another occasion, in the book section of a charity shop, an elderly woman whispered furtively, 'Are you a priest?' and then poured out, in whispers, a story of years of feeling rejected by the Roman Catholic Church. 'It is nothing they say, just that all I ever see is men up front and women kept in the pews. I can't believe I've met a priest who is a woman like me.' I don't think I had anticipated how, simply by being an ordained woman, I would offer other women an opportunity to know themselves beloved by God.

In my first year at seminary my spiritual director, a priest on the faculty, helped me to explore being British in a foreign culture. One day she surprised me by saying she was sure that I would return to Britain, and that one gift I would take would be the experience of ordination and ministry without an emphasis on my gender. In 1999 I did return to the UK and now train people for ordination. I soon discovered that at the course much hung on my arrival, as the women students were impatient for an ordained woman on staff. Suddenly my gender was significant in a way that was new to me. I was taken aback when students wept in joy after I presided, and when several told me that this was the first time they had seen a woman preside. These were people about to be ordained who had not experienced the ordained ministry of women. One said, 'When I saw you there I finally realized that God really has called me and I need not be ashamed to be a woman', while another spoke of her now-allayed fears that ordination would mean sacrificing her femininity in order to survive. I realize that amid my questions about ordination, these particular issues never arose because I had so many role models. A man wrote to me to recount his journey from opposition to the ordination of women when he started training, to the joy of finally receiving the bread and wine from me. We can often forget that the ordination of women gives a reciprocal gift to men – the gift that was previously exclusive to women of receiving priestly ministry from people of the other gender.

Many conversations with students are about practical issues for women in ministry – from clergy blouses to women's support networks – questions that most cannot ask their male incumbents. In interviews, I ask students about their role models as they prepare for ordination. Many are initially surprised at the question, but then the men have no trouble answering, while women often only name men, or, when pressed to name a woman, say 'the vicar's wife'. It is at times like this that I realize, in a way I did not in the USA, what a gift the ordained women I knew were to me and what we who are ordained offer without realizing it. It is wonderful to hear young girls say, 'When I grow up I want to be a priest like you', knowing that they need not be disappointed.

For many in the parishes I visit on Sundays I am the first ordained woman they have met, simply because their incumbent is a man. I know from subsequent conversations that women in these churches are no different from the women buying petrol and in the charity shop. At root we yearn to know ourselves as truly created in the image of God, and it is both humbling and a joy to share the moment of recognition when this need is partially satisfied by seeing priests who are 'women like me'. But this should not be – ordination is not necessary for people to know they are created in the image of God. However, in the last ten years ordination is being freed, finally, from sending terrible subliminal messages about the relative goodness of being a man or woman, and it is a stunning privilege to be a part of that.

I never set out to be a role model and have hardly been a pioneer. But now that I am back in England, I understand the wisdom behind those words that snowy afternoon in Connecticut. My experience there gives me hope that in time the fidelity of those who paved the way here will bear the fruit of an ordained ministry where the priest's gender goes unremarked, yet brings its own particular gifts, a ministry that enables all people to live in freedom as God's people in God's world.

* * *

After 16 years as a town planner Rosalind Brown moved to the United States to join a religious community of men and women in the diocese of Pittsburgh. With their encouragement she was ordained after training at Yale Divinity School. She was vicar of a church near Pittsburgh before moving to Salisbury in 1999, where she divides her time between the Ordained Local Ministry Scheme and STETS (Southern Theological Education and Training Scheme) and wonders how she ever had doubts about ordination. She is the author of several prize-winning hymn texts and, with Christopher Cocksworth, of *Being a Priest Today* (Canterbury Press, 2002).

Fulfilling Vocation: Continuing Campaign

JANE SHAW

I first had a vocation to the priesthood when I was 16. I saw that a friend's father combined a dual vocation as scholar and priest, and somehow I had an inkling that I might have that dual calling too. It was 1979. I do not know what gave me the extraordinary idea that I could be ordained, but I certainly felt a sense of outrage that I might 'not' be able to be ordained. That year the Movement for the Ordination of Women (MOW) was formed and I joined immediately. My activist career began. My parish priest invited women priests from the Episcopal Church in the United States to come and preach. At an age when most teenage girls were screaming at pop stars, I was queuing up for the autograph of Canon Mary Michael Simpson who was visiting from the Cathedral of St John the Divine in New York!

As an undergraduate at Oxford, I was reading history, but my real interest was in the campaign for the ordination of women. I remained active with MOW. I was lucky too in that in Oxford there were informal feminist liturgy and theology groups. They became an important lifeline to me, a young undergraduate who was taught entirely by men and did not learn anything about women's history in my formal studies. I was doing my own research on the history of women in the Church, and also busily campaigning, and in 1984 – when the issue went to Synod – I did a lot of work in the press and on television. The defeat of that motion was a defining moment for many, not least my feminist father who had always been involved in the Church but at that moment resigned as church warden and did not return to any active participation in church life until after 1994 when women were ordained as priests.

Meanwhile, I went to America for the first time, saw Edwina

Sandys' sculpture of the 'Christa' figure hanging in the Cathedral of St John the Divine and met as many women priests as I could. On finishing my degree at Oxford, I went to Harvard Divinity School. There, my world was opened up. I received a broad, inspiring theological education from some of the best scholars in their field, who were thoroughly aware of how issues such as gender and ethnicity shape both ideas and institutions. I count myself very fortunate indeed. Of course, my faith was intellectually pulled apart – and I think that's not a bad thing! My faith was put back together at a different level altogether, through worship in a community and daily use of the prayer book. This happened at two places – the Society of St John the Divine, the Cowley Fathers' monastery in Cambridge, Massachusetts, a dynamic, prayerful and socially active monastic community, thoroughly supportive of women priests; and then at Church Divinity School of the Pacific, the Episcopal seminary where I taught while doing my PhD in history at UC Berkeley.

I returned to England, to teach at Oxford, in 1994, the year that women were first ordained as priests. In fact, I came back in April as those first ordinations were happening. Many people had asked me about ordination while I was living in the States, but I had always held off, saying that I would know when the time was right. The time not only became right, but pressing, in 1996. Despite the fact that this was 16 years after my initial sense of call, and despite (or perhaps because of!) my long activist history, I still felt a resistance to 'signing up' to the institutional Church in this way. I remember walking round the University Parks every lunch time, having earnest debates with God. I finally took myself off to the Diocesan Director of Ordinands – with whom I had been meeting for nearly two years – and he just seemed relieved that I was now willing to have this long-standing vocation tested. I was accepted for ordination and was ordained deacon in 1997, priest in 1998, and served my title as non-stipendiary minister at the University Church. Nineteen years after first sensing that I might be called to be a scholar-priest, I became one, and it is an immense privilege. Last year I moved from a purely teaching post to one which combines teaching with running a large chapel and pastoral work – as dean of divinity, chaplain and fellow at New College, Oxford. I am New College's first female dean of divinity in its 623-year history. Both the college and the chapel community have been immensely supportive of me, and rather proud of themselves for being the first major Oxbridge choral foundation to appoint a woman as dean of chapel.

My generation owes a huge debt to the many laywomen who campaigned for the ordination of women as priests, knowing that it would never happen in time for them to offer themselves for ordination, and to the ordained men who stuck their necks out in a frequently hostile Church to support us. I am glad to be able to record for posterity the names of some of that older generation who supported and encouraged me and, often without knowing it, were my role models. They are (in roughly chronological order!): Jack Shaw, David L. Edwards, David Sharp, Joan Diment, Alan and Margaret Webster, Kathryn Ross, Penny Nairne, Rusty Page, Monica Furlong, Vincent Strudwick and Bob Jeffery.

As a child of a feminist father (the most important of all those supporters) I am aware that we always have work to do for greater justice for women and all those who have been marginalized by the churches and society. At this moment, as I am about to turn 40, I can thank God for all that I have been fortunate enough to do, for all whom I have met in my faith journey and for all that has been achieved in bringing about the justice of which the Gospels speak, but I look forward to the work yet to be done, in and out of the churches, for greater equality for all.

*   *   *

Jane Shaw is dean of divinity, chaplain and fellow of New College, Oxford. Prior to that, she was tutorial fellow in ecclesiastical history at Regent's Park College, Oxford. She is also a chaplain at Christ Church Cathedral, Oxford. She preaches and lectures regularly in the USA and is professor of historical theology at the Graduate Theological Foundation, Indiana. She writes on modern religious history and has a forthcoming book on miracles in Enlightenment England, with Yale University Press. She was educated at Oxford, Harvard and the University of California at Berkeley. She is vice-chair of national WATCH and a theological consultant to the House of Bishops.

Vocation as a Journey of Discovery

FIONA STEWART-DARLING

As I reflect on my journey towards ordination to the priesthood and beyond, it has been punctuated by many intellectual, spiritual and emotional somersaults. I grew up in a tradition within the Church of England whose language centred on vicar and curate. Until I began my journey in testing my vocation with the Diocesan Director of Ordinands, I was exploring becoming a deaconess, which for me had been the best kept secret of the Church of England. It had taken years to discover what my vocation was, and it certainly was not the initial option suggested to me, the mission field.

However, as I explored further my vocation the goalposts kept moving – as soon as I got my head around the idea of becoming a deaconess, women were being ordained deacon. At my ACCM interview I was asked if I had a calling to the priesthood. In less than 12 months I had discovered a whole new side to the Church. What was God calling me to be? What was a deacon? What was a priest? Suddenly from being a vocational calling to serve the Church I discovered as I entered theological college, it was more like preparing to run through a minefield.

I found myself having to do a lot of emotional, spiritual and intellectual gymnastics, to move from a position of not having the word 'priest' in my church vocabulary, to finding out what it meant to be a priest and to discover whether I, as a woman, could really be so bold as to imagine that this was God's calling for me. With much heart-searching, studying of the scriptures and listening to all the arguments for and against, the sense of God's calling to be ordained a priest grew ever deeper within me. I struggled with how could God be so cruel as to call me to do something which was in conflict with the Church. I found, as the vote of 11 November 1992 grew closer, I was able to share my own journey to the point where I believed that there was no theological reason why women could not be priests and how I believed I too had a vocation to be one. This journey was very important for me as the opposition became more heated. I found myself saying to people, let me tell you my story and share with you my own journey. The pressure as a curate knowing that the whole of women's ministry within the parish was judged by the way I behaved and went about doing my job, was very hard.

Yet the years and months of waiting accumulated into one day. As I thought about what I wanted to write for this book, I read through the two scrapbooks I have. One contains the story of my journey through selection to priesthood, and the other contains articles, newspaper cuttings and letters I received following the 11 November vote.

One of the memories from 11 November was sitting in the refectory in the basement of Church House, Westminster. The number of votes was announced and everyone in their nervousness was unable to do the calculations. Then when the Archbishop announced that the motion had been carried, there was initially a stunned silence. No one knew what anybody else's views were except those of friends around each of us. Were we in among those who were in favour or anti? I remember thinking I had a strategy if the vote failed, but did not know how to react in the event of it being passed. The room then erupted in sheer joy – it was a truly overwhelming moment. At last the Church was willing to accept that women, too, had a genuine calling by God to the priesthood, reflecting the complete equality of humanity.

I was very struck by the interest taken by people outside the Church. Another memory of that was walking along Great Smith Street with another female deacon after the initial elation had died down. We were stopped by a man who was a complete stranger in a pinstriped suit and rolled umbrella, etc. He asked us the result of the vote and when we told him, was overjoyed and spontaneously hugged us both.

The letters in the scrapbook reminded me of the number of parishioners in the Church where I served my title and was eventually ordained priest, who had done a U-turn on their views of the ordination of women to the priesthood. We were a large parish with a number of stipendiary clergy. One of my colleagues was against women becoming priests, as was his wife. They had always treated me warmly. On the day of the vote I had a card from them, which said, 'whatever the outcome tomorrow, we shall always value, and appreciate your ministry, and give thanks for your friendship'. When I was ordained priest they gave me a cathedral surplice, which I treasure. Some years later after I left the parish I had a letter to say that they both had now accepted holy communion from a woman and were happy to do so.

The acceptance of women into the priesthood began with the vote in General Synod and continued through the first women ordained priest in 1994, of which I had the privilege of being one. For me it has been an ongoing journey, as clergy colleagues have supported us and others have changed their minds, as congregations have experienced our ministry, so, too, we have discovered together more of the richness and diversity we bring to the body of Christ. My journey began by throwing my perceptions of God and my view of the scriptures into question. It has continued to challenge my perceptions of God and taught me once again to be open to the scriptures and not only to come with years of tradition and preconceived ideas. Finally, at the end of the day, it is God and humanity that we serve, and the most important thing is how we bring God's love and the gospel to other people. The journey of discovery continues.

* * *

Fiona Stewart-Darling was born in 1958, and initially studied chemistry and worked for British Gas as a senior scientist. She was trained at Trinity College, Bristol, ordained deacon in 1991, and priest in 1994. Fiona served her title in the Cotswolds in the parish of Cirencester. She then became the assistant chaplain at Cheltenham and Gloucester College of Higher Education (now the University of Gloucestershire). She has been in her present post as university chaplain at the University of Portsmouth since 1997. She is also an honorary chaplain at the cathedral. Fiona adds: 'My latest hobby (for those interested) is kite flying. What else do you do living by the sea in a very windy city?'

Women: Beautifully and Wonderfully Made in the Image of God

ROSE HUDSON-WILKIN

I grew up in the Anglican Church in the 1960s at a time when it was still known as the 'Church of England in Jamaica'. In fact the priest I was baptized by at six months old and who served the cure for several more years – well into my teens – was an expatriate, Archdeacon Price. I have a vivid memory of him – perhaps because of his bushy eyebrows. My family worshipped regularly at the main service that began at 7.30am at the parish church, which was approximately five or six miles away. We children attended the local mission that was just across the road from where we lived. St Francis Mission was the place where my faith in God was nurtured. The Church Army, Captains Daniel, Braham and Kerr staffed the mission. They led morning prayer twice a month and were responsible on a day-to-day level. The priest came fortnightly and celebrated the sacraments.

At the age of 14 I was going through a particular crisis in my life. Although my parents' generation 'fed' and 'watered' us, they were never tactile. I guess the bottom line was that I felt unloved. It was at that time that I can remember my friend at school, Janice, who was a year above me, speaking at a Student Christian Movement meeting about a 'God who loved us so much that he gave his only son to die for us'. At that moment I remember thinking, 'If God loved me that much, then I would serve him.' My life took on a new meaning. From then on worship became something that I enjoyed. I eagerly looked forward to saying canticles like the 'Te Deum' – a song of praise to God. My call to a vocation to full-time ministry was born at that time. There was no flashing light. I just knew.

My dilemma was vocation to which ministry? I knew there were no women priests even though the debate was not current (at least in Jamaica). I had heard that there were deaconesses, and once I had met a female Church Army Sister – Sister Norma. Because we always had a Church Army Captain, I had some limited knowledge of that ministry. I continued through high school still with a burning desire to be a 'minister'. After achieving my 'O' levels, I decided to leave school, as my family could not afford to keep me on. I worked for a year as a pre-trained teacher at a school in rural St James. While there I applied to the diocese of Jamaica to be trained as a Church Army Officer. I was accepted and along with three others set off for my training in England at the age of 18.

After completing the three-year course, I returned to Jamaica where I worked in the newly created Christian Education Department. This work took me closer to rural parishes, which had no resident priests. These were places of worship filled with women that, although they had competent lay leadership, were denied the sacraments because there was no one with 'male genitalia' to administer it. It was then that I began to ask questions of those in charge at the various deanery meetings, etc., as to why women, clearly exercising competent leadership and who were deeply committed to the faith, were not being allowed to test their vocation to the priesthood. This was also the period that saw my own vocation to the priesthood deepening.

I returned to live in England and offered myself to be trained as a deacon. Those interviewing on behalf of the Church did not appear to be overjoyed at welcoming a young and committed black woman to its orders. It was suggested to me that I needed to look after my family (husband plus one child) instead.

I did not give up and eventually was accepted by another diocese, to which we had moved. I have vivid memories of standing outside Church House at the Synod debate in November 1992, holding a placard with the words, 'Women, Beautifully and Wonderfully Made in the Image of God'.

There were times during the day when I wished that I was inside the chambers contributing to that debate. As the various speakers were called, I could feel my stomach churning – it was like being on a roller-coaster. It was at the end of the vote that I realized how lucky I was to have been standing outside instead of being in the chambers. Those inside were told that they had to receive the vote in silence. There were no such restrictions outside. We hugged each other. We sang and praised God, that at last, the Church was listening to the Holy Spirit.

My own ordination to the priesthood came on 23 April 1994. The weeks leading up to it were momentous. I had a party for my daughter who was celebrating her sixth birthday. That afternoon I left for Bristol Cathedral where I attended the very first priesting of women in England. It was an amazing experience – history in the making. That night as we drove back to the Midlands, there was a more sombre mood. I had a funeral to prepare for – I had been informed days before that my father had died, so there was just enough time to get packed and head to Heathrow for my flight to Jamaica. There were only two weeks to do everything before getting back for my ordination retreat.

The day of my ordination was a 'Simeon' experience. There was a feeling of fulfilment that words are inadequate to describe. When pushed, I describe it as being pregnant and giving birth. The long gestation, then the joy and pain in the birthing process. My own personal joy was very strong, but I was acutely aware of feeling the pain of the women who had tried to be obedient to the word of God but who were not allowed to respond to their call and be priests in God's Church.

Eight years after my own ordination to the priesthood, I thank God for the number of people who have approached me and said that through my ministry, they were now sure that God had called women. One man whose mother I had buried insisted to the undertakers that he wanted me to do his wife's funeral even though he was miles away from my parish. He later told me, 'When we spoke on the phone, I didn't know you were black. My mother didn't like black people, nor did she like women priests. It was such a beautiful service though, that I just knew I had to have you for my wife's funeral.' He further added, 'When I came to see you, you hugged me. If a man had done that I would have thumped him.'

There are those still who refuse to have me minister to them on the grounds that I am both female and black. This is painful. I handle these moments by acknowledging the pain but being fully aware that 'the loss is theirs not mine'. I continue in my ministry, confident that, not only am I called to represent Christ, but that I am beautifully and wonderfully made in the image of God.

* * *

Rose Hudson-Wilkin was born in Montego Bay, Jamaica and was educated there at primary and secondary level. She then left for England to be trained as a Church Army officer. On completing her training Rose returned to Jamaica and worked in the newly established Christian Education Department with lay training as her main focus.

She later returned to England and was ordained to the diaconate in 1991. She served her curacy in St Matthew's, Wolverhampton, and was ordained to the priesthood in 1994. Rose worked part time as a diocesan officer in the Lichfield diocese as the Officer for Black Anglican Concerns and part time as associate priest in the Church of the Good Shepherd, West Bromwich. She is presently the vicar of the united benefice of Holy Trinity with St Phillip, Dalston, and All Saints, Haggerston.

She is a member of the Broadcasting Standards Commission (BSC) and chairs the national Committee for Minority Ethnic Anglican Concerns and the Worldwide Committee for SPCK.

She is married with three children. Her hobbies include reading, tennis, scrabble, entertaining and travelling. She is also interested in issues relating to matters of justice and the indiginization of the gospel.

Recognizing Gifts

LESLEY BENTLEY

As a young child I can remember looking across our church one Sunday to see, with surprise, a woman dressed like a nun sitting in the congregation. She turned out to be deaconess Winifred Cooke who had retired and come to live in Nottingham and to worship with us at St Wilfrid's.

The deaconess order had been newly revived in the 1880s, and Deaconess Cooke was a member of this order. She lived an almost ascetic lifestyle in an inner city area of Nottingham. She had lived a hard life, more undervalued than valued, but still carried with her the love of her calling. She was delighted when I first started to talk of a calling as a deaconess, but then became confused and disappointed when at the age of 19 I married, because she believed that this would rule out my vocation. I think at that time it did, as deaconesses were still not allowed to marry.

Now, 20 years after my ordination as deaconess in Derby Cathedral, my vocation has taken me somewhere that she could never have envisaged. I am team rector designate of one of the largest parishes in the diocese of Ripon and Leeds, currently with a staff of team vicar designate, an NSM, a reader and a deacon in training. This demonstrates how my calling has been recognized by the Church in a way that hers never could have been at that time.

My journey in Christian ministry has been an exciting one, with some disappointments, but with a strong sense of the Holy Spirit working within the Church so that the gifts of its people could be recognized. I think it is no accident that the development of the public ministry of women within the Church has been accompanied by the recognition of the gifts of all, and a move towards collaborative ministry. Here at St John and St Luke's the pastoral ministry groups, the youth and children's groups, the nurture groups and the late evening service all have lay leadership.

One of the most exciting days in my ministry was to act as host to a lunch for the female bishops of the Anglican Communion at the last Lambeth Conference. The lunch was organized by the Deans/Advisers in Women's Ministry of the Church of England. This is known as NADAWM, and I was chairperson at the time. We wanted a quiet time together, away from the blare of the Lambeth publicity, and over lunch we asked the bishops to tell us the stories of their calling. I was moved by the quiet authority with which they spoke, an authority in which status had no place, only a sense of God's calling. There were stories of struggle and pain alongside stories of strong and deep support.

My own calling to public ministry began in my late teens, but it was in my early twenties that I candidated for ministry from the Church of St John the Evangelist in Mickleover, Derby. This church put a strong emphasis on lay ministry, and lay people were enabled to take real responsibility within the church community. Over a four-year period the church produced three female candidates for public ministry, plus a fourth woman who had grown up in the parish and candidated for ministry at the same time, but from a different church.

I think that I had a relatively easy journey as my ministry developed, meeting only small amounts of misunderstanding and opposition. When I knocked nervously on the door of my first funeral visit I was met by a confused look, and the statement, ' . . . but the undertakers have already called this morning.' 'Yes,' I replied, 'but I am here because I am taking your husband's service.' The fact that the Church of England minister could be female was clearly beyond comprehension. On another occasion I visited one of the few families that I ever encountered who refused to have a female take a funeral service. By the end of my visit they had changed things round, and said, 'It is a real pity we have asked for a man to take this service. We would like you.' We changed the arrangements and I was later invited back to bury another family member.

Expressions of real support have been greater. Canon Law stated that a deaconess could only baptize in the absence of a priest, so one of my vicars offered to hide in a cupboard in the vestry when I was due to baptize. Following the Synod vote that accepted the ordination of women as priests, I was stopped in the street by people anxious to say what a good thing this would be. Indeed, people are surprised that women are still unable to become bishops in the Church of England.

We now live in Harrogate. Odd to think that when Synod debated the issue of women priests my husband was on a conference in Harrogate, actually staying within the parish of St John and St Luke. When the vote came through he tearfully ordered a double vodka and tonic from a startled hotel room service. Deaconess Cooke didn't normally drink vodka, but I believe that she too might have been tempted that day.

*   *   *

Lesley Bentley celebrated 20 years of public ministry this year, having been made deaconess by the Bishop of Derby in 1982 before being made priest with the first group of female candidates in the Liverpool diocese. She has served as curate in three parishes, one with responsibility for a daughter church and as incumbent in two, one of which was a Local Ecumenical Partnership. As Dean of Women's Ministry for the Liverpool diocese she also chaired the National Association of Diocesan Advisers in Women's Ministry (1997–2001). In 1985 she pioneered maternity leave for stipendiary deaconesses. She is now team rector designate of St John and St Luke, Bilton in the diocese of Ripon and Leeds.

A Journey of Awe and Grace

MARY HUSTON

I feel a little like Paul when he described himself as 'one untimely born' (1 Corinthians 15:8), speaking of his own call to be the latest apostle after Peter and the disciples. I was out of the country when the process leading to the passing of the measure to ordain women was at its height. I was back in time to watch the pictures, the scenes of celebration at Church House on the news, and subsequent ordinations, but it seemed to have nothing to do with me. Because I had only recently arrived back in England, I was spending most of my time trying to earn a living and overcome the peculiar form of bereavement reverse culture shock can take.

It was some time later that an idea that would not go away finally propelled me to speak to my vicar, in the hope that I could get it out of my system, and I could get on with the rest of my life. I should have known better; he advised me to explore the ordination process further.

So I started out on the journey which saw me on the Saturday before I was ordained deacon, in an absolute panic. I talked myself into and out of going through with it all so many times I lost count. Taking myself by the scruff of the neck, I decided that my strategy would be to go to the Sunday morning service where I was to serve my title, and in an anonymous way, 'get the feel' of the place and so diffuse my terror. My plan unravelled almost immediately, as one of the church wardens whom I had met some months earlier, was on vigilant duty at the back of the church. My anonymity did not last long, but at least my fear diminished enough to make it through the ordination service.

Three and a half years later, as I come to the end of my curacy, and reflect on my own experience and that of those on the receiving end of my ministry, I offer four words: laughter, puzzlement, bereavement and awe.

Whether it has been the laughter of celebration at a baptism or
a wedding, or the suppressed laughter at the unexpected arrival
at the offertory on Christmas morning of a flagon filled, not with
wine but soapy water, its presence has made a huge difference.
Children have often been a significant part of this. I struggled
with an unexpected primary school assembly where I asked the
question 'What was the first Christmas present?' to be told that
it was chocolate. I managed to establish that the right answer
was in fact 'Jesus' (clue being 'Five letters beginning with J'), I
then asked, 'What did Jesus come wrapped in?' (We had begun
by talking about Christmas presents.) A silence ensued, broken
by a very young theologian who said simply, 'His mother.' Sheer
genius; the incarnation in a nutshell, and much laughter all
round.

So what of puzzlement? Certainly I have puzzled with the
questions, 'Why me and why now?'; 'Why me in this particular
conversation or crisis?'; 'Am I doing or saying the right thing?'
Sometimes, too, it has been about dealing with the puzzlement of
others. I applied to serve as a governor at a local school and
arrived at the meeting where it would be decided whether I
was to be elected or not. Invited to say a few words as to why I
wanted to be a governor, I stumbled my way through my CV
to a group of people who clearly were not sure what I was, and
possibly might have been struggling with their image of Anglican
women priests as role-modelled by Dawn French. They still
seemed puzzled when I had finished, but they did decide to give
me a chance, which has meant my gaining some valuable skills
and new friends.

Yet in spite of much joy and fun, inevitably there have been
darker moments. Not long after I was ordained deacon, I felt a
cloud hanging over me. Nothing seemed to be wrong, yet life did
not ring right. I could not put my finger on it, until I realized one
day that I was grieving. I had spent years learning skills as a nurse
and midwife and felt that I had lost them, or that they no longer
had any use. Had I wasted my time?

What healed me was a visit to someone who had just been
diagnosed with early breast cancer. Fortunately, she was able to
enter treatment quickly and had surgery and chemotherapy. I
visited her at home to take her communion and found myself
praying with her, speaking together about where God was in all

of this, and then being asked to check that her wound was healing well. Call me thick, but it was one of those moments of clarity when all the pieces landed in the right place, and I realized I was actually in the job I was supposed to be in after all.

Which brings me to awe. I still find it an awesome thing standing in front of a congregation, seeking in some way to communicate God to them. Perhaps it has been at its most extreme when taking the funeral of someone who has died too young, and trying to find some words of hope to offer, wondering if anything can reach past such awful sadness. I have been touched that, even in that most desolate of places, when I have felt at my most inadequate, God has met me and those for whom in that moment, I am called to care. I hope it is a sense of awe and sheer grace that I will never lose, as a priest or as a human being.

*   *   *

Mary Huston was born in August 1959, the eldest of two children. Brought up and educated in Doncaster, South Yorkshire, she left to study at Hull University graduating with a BA in theology. She trained as a nurse and midwife at St Mary's hospital, London, and undertook further studies in tropical diseases nursing before travelling to Paraguay to work with the indigenous peoples of the Chaco. On return to England in 1992 she worked as a practice nurse and pastoral worker before beginning ordination training with the South East Institute of Theological Education. She was ordained in 1998 and is currently stipendiary curate at St Stephen's, South Dulwich, in the diocese of Southwark.

Following the Spirit: Risk as Obedience

ALYSON PEBERDY

It's Good Friday and I've introduced another new service, 'the Tree of Life'. The children are proudly, but rather too noisily, displaying their artwork. Some of the older members of the congregation, hoping for silence, are looking uncomfortable. I'm feeling tense. It's been a lot of effort and now, in tiredness and self-doubt, I feel I've taken one risk too many. Until we come to the mime.

In seconds everyone falls quiet. The absorbed faces of the children carrying stones around the Church are infectious. In their intensely focused actions they begin to speak for us all. Although the stones being carried are heavy and weighing us down they have become part of who we are. Then slowly, sadly, reluctantly the stones are put down at the foot of the cross. The atmosphere is empty and heavy until suddenly one of the children looks under the cross and notices some flowering branches. With immense dignity and grace the children begin to improvise a dance holding the branches aloft. Stuck in our pews we gaze up at the budding and flowering twigs leading our eyes tentatively, then joyfully, in circling sweeps around the church. At the end we are led out into the sun. Young and old, black and white, male and female, happy and sad, we rise up from the pews and quietly follow towards the joy of Easter.

It wasn't one risk too many, though it might have been. I'm reminded yet again of the lesson I keep learning, forgetting and needing to relearn. Whenever I try to please people instead of following the inner risky promptings of the Spirit, I lose sight of my vocation.

I was 49 when ordained priest and I rejoice in the freedom of being too old to be seduced by the lure of rising up the 'hierarchy'. Whatever difference I make needs to be here and now as a parish priest in South London. And yet I have been slow to find my feet. Why? Partly because the Church of England is facing major financial cuts.

Almost three years ago I moved from a curacy in a friendly and supportive team in Berkshire to become vicar of a single parish in south-east London. Of course there are neighbouring parishes, but one is 'Forward in Faith' and the other two fell vacant quite soon after I arrived. I quickly had to learn to work in a far more isolated environment than I would choose. Then I was asked by the bishop (though the parishes themselves were not consulted) to become interim priest-in-charge of the two vacant parishes. One parish was planning a new church building and the other was facing the possibility of closure. The administrative work-load was enormous and the pastoral and staffing complexities overwhelming. I resigned from one after a year and the second after two years.

With enormous relief and some sadness at achieving so little I've put down the heavy weight of an impossible task. Now I look forward with anticipation and hope to leading my parish forward into God's future, however many risks that will involve, and I suspect there may be many.

* * *

Alyson Peberdy was ordained priest in 1997, serving her title in the new Windsor team ministry. In 1999 she became vicar of St Saviour's, Brockley Hill. Before ordination Alyson worked as research fellow and lecturer in health and social welfare at the Open University, Milton Keynes, and was also national vice-moderator of the Movement for the Ordination of Women. She is married with two adult children.

It Doesn't Hurt a Bit

ENID MORGAN

It was to be a 'first' in a little country church in West Wales that had never before had a woman priest to celebrate. I had been warned that the number one organist was keeping away, but that number two had agreed to stand in. Feeling rather jumpy, I made a final check at the desk and noticed an elderly couple come in. Then the man marched back towards the door. I groaned inwardly – but he had only gone to get a hymn book. As I greeted people at the end of the service, along came the hymn book seeker. He was tall, with a ramrod, military gait, and I stood a little straighter to greet him. He shook my hand and remarked easily, 'First time we've had a woman celebrate, y'know. Excellent! It didn't hurt a bit!'

In the Province of Wales, with its six dioceses and about as many clergy as the diocese of Oxford, women were ordained deacons in 1976. But we wallowed in the wake of the English debate, less familiar with party conflicts than the Church of England. It was not until September 1995 that the Governing Body (our General Synod) gathered together the required two-thirds majority in the house of clergy. Once the 90+ women waiting for ordination to the priesthood were ordained at Epiphany 1996, people discovered that the Eucharist celebrated by the women was the same Eucharist as before. The very familiarity of the rite helped. The men who had supported the ordination of women exclaimed at the 'ordinariness' of it, as though we had all somehow expected it to be different. For some of the women there was even a sense of let-down that it wasn't transformed. For the new ministers of the sacrament were subsumed by the sacrament itself, the words spoken now by women's voices, the actions with women's initially tentative grace. So the experience of becoming priests was of relief, of shedding the burden of being a problem, of stepping out of a cramped cage and being able to stand up straight.

Coming together as women deacons was always full of merriment – slightly edgy at times. There were always funny stories to tell, the genuinely funny as well as the ones that would otherwise make you weep. There was the young woman deacon who had turned up in an orthopaedics ward in the hospital to give communion to a young man hurt in a car accident. She was greeted with howls of laughter, and the young man confessed shamefacedly to having thought she was a Kissogram. There was the oddity of a woman in a dog-collar dismissed with, 'Well you look quite normal from there down.' The visiting deacon who apologized for not being the vicar was told, 'Don't you worry, love. I shan't have to put in my teeth for you!'; and the slightly embarrassed face of the man at the vicarage door when told, 'But I *am* the vicar.'

After ordination to the diaconate in 1984 (I was 44 at the time) I worked for two years as a curate and seven as that self-contradictory phenomenon, a 'deacon-in-charge'. It led, surprisingly, to an ecclesiastical bureaucrat post as Director of Mission for the province. (The imposing title disguised the work of an executive secretary to the Board of Mission, an institution held in deep suspicion not only by the diocesan clergy, but by most of the bishops at the time.) To go from a deacon-in-charge trying to keep her head down and get on with it, to an upfront job trying to work with the bishops was a jolt. It was a difficult 'first woman' situation in which 'I must not fail', but a post in which no one could actually succeed. Worst of all for me personally was that when in 1996 I was ordained priest, my job didn't really need a priest. Hence in 2000 I returned to parish ministry, this time in the diocese of Llandaf and without my hands tied behind my back.

Reflecting on my own story I have become more and more convinced that the accusation of women being driven by a secular feminist agenda is quite spurious. All women's lives have been affected by feminism and any woman who goes to university or casts a vote has no right to be embarrassed by the word. But the opposition to women in positions of authority matches attitudes in other professions. Vocation as it is, priesthood is organized, at least in part, as a profession. In the police force, in medicine, in the law and in business women are resented and perceived as a threat. In all these spheres there are men who cannot bear that women should be able to do what they most value for themselves. In the Church, evangelicals don't want women to teach and preach and bear authority, and Anglo-Catholics baulk at seeing a woman at the altar. It is a common psychological feature, but it is wretched theology.

Once ordained, being a priest, and getting on with the job as well as accepting the condition, the difficulties and rewards are much as they are for the men. They have to do with what George Herbert called in his time 'seeing man in need and God despised'. It is about casting oneself wholeheartedly into prayer and service, into studying, learning, organizing and even (despised word) managing. It is allowing Christ to dwell in one and realizing that you are a focus through which people are helped to find God.

As the years go by I see, too, the challenge of being a contradiction to the assumptions and norms of society. The Church no longer sets the agenda – indeed it is scoffed at. But we must, in our sin and frailty, keep pointing to Christ by word and deed and presence. We must ward off the arthritics of bitterness and old age by laughter – warm, compassionate and irresistible, and hope that it is the laughter of heaven at the heavy weather we make of things.

*   *   *

Enid Morgan is vicar of Llangynwyd with Maesteg in the diocese of Llandaf and honorary canon in Llandaf Cathedral.

The Best Section of the Best Branch

JUDITH MALTBY

Anglicans are very good at self-deprecation, so it is important to remember that many people (including a number in this collection of essays) have chosen to express their Christian faith in the Anglican tradition. I, however, am not one of them, A 'cradle' Anglican, my faith nurtured by committed lay parents and dedicated Anglo-Catholic parish priests (largely in the happily named 'Biretta Belt' of the mid-western Episcopal Church in the USA), not being an Anglican has never really been an option for me. In over 40 years, I have had times of alienation from either God or the Church (more the latter than the former and not the same thing, of course, though sometimes mistaken for each other). But the thought of 'going elsewhere', apart from a brief flirtation with Roman Catholicism in adolescence, which is something I suspect most people raised Anglo-Catholic go through at some point or other – has never really been in my emotional or intellectual physics. As Rose Macaulay's protagonist puts it in her great novel of Anglican angst, *The Towers of Trebizond*: 'I am high, even extreme, but somewhat lapsed, which is a sound position. as you belong to the best section of the best branch of the Christian Church. but seldom attend its services' (Rose Macaulay, *The Towers of Trebizond* (1956, repr. 1986), p. 7).

An odd culture to produce and nurture a vocation to the priesthood? Perhaps. But what is good about the Catholic tradition in Anglicanism at its best: a eucharistic spirituality which is fundamentally Christocentric; an engagement with scripture disciplined by a lectionary and the rhythms of the church year – a conviction that the material is infused with and can convey divinity; a belief that worship is both hard work and bags of fun; a sense that history (albeit sometimes romanticized) matters – these are things which provided a nurturing and empowering Christian faith for me.

What, then, first enabled me to question in the 1970s the status quo prohibition on women in the priesthood? Truth to tell (and this is a sobering reflection for any activist or educator), it was *not* any of the arguments I heard put in favour. These seemed to my pious adolescent ears a mere application of 'secular' conceptions of justice (never doubting, of course, that as a woman I had every right to vote, own property and go to university) to what was indisputably 'sacred', the priesthood. That may seem odd as, thanks to my parents, especially my mother, I had never doubted that just as racism was sinful in society, so it was an equal, shameful evil in the Church – perhaps even *more* sinful because we Christians are supposed to operate to higher standards. My mother had become an Episcopalian from Lutheranism as a teenager inspired by the example and ministry of a courageous Anglo-Catholic priest, the future Bishop of Western Michigan, Father Bennison, in part by his stand in the early 1950s in desegregating his parish church in Joliet, Illinois. So the Anglo-Catholic commitment to the social gospel, rather than how many inches of lace on a cotta, took precedence in my childhood theological formation, thank goodness. But as for women priests (including women of colour), *that* was, for some reason, 'different'.

Ironically, it was the very theological tools given to me by my Anglo-Catholic upbringing which allowed the questions to come. Essential in this process was my undergraduate chaplain and his wife, Timothy and Mary Hallett, at the Chapel of St John the Divine at the University of Illinois. They taught me and continue to teach me many things, but crucially at the age of 19 or 20 they helped me to see that a critical engagement with one's faith tradition is the best form of commitment to it. For example, in the 1970s, I was hearing for the first time from those opposed that we were supposed to think of the priest 'as Christ' whereas I knew perfectly well that in the Eucharist, Christ was 'located' in the sacred elements. One didn't genuflect to the priest carrying the host, but to the host! Get a grip, so to speak, I remember thinking with all the assurance of a college sophomore. (We were always, I should say, Prayer Book Catholics.) I had been raised on a piety which emphasized the incarnation and therefore *identification* with the sufferings of Christ (both ours for his and his for ours) on the cross, rather than *substitution*. So, if Jesus' maleness was more significant, in short, *matters* more, than his humanity – but men and women are equal, as opponents like to say, despite the breathtaking departure from 'tradition' such a statement represents – *what* was half the human race to make of Good Friday? What then, was Good Friday to me? That old prohibition began to look pretty unCatholic.

I have said little about the past ten years since the vote or the past eight years as a priest or how a kid from the Mid-West ended up being ordained to the priesthood in 1994 by the Bishop of Oxford. In a nutshell, unable to proceed in the ordination process in 1979 because of the opposition to the ordination of women by the then Bishop of Springfield, I took the opportunity offered to go to Cambridge to work on a PhD in church history. It was only going to be for three years but, as they say, one thing led to another. I have now lived in England and with the Church of England longer than I have lived in America and with the Episcopal Church. I am very much 'at home' here, though still prone occasionally to what I think of as 'Episcopalian moments' especially in discussions about the secretive and untransparent way our bishops are chosen in the Church of England. I have chilled out a lot, leaving behind the triumphalist Anglo-Catholicism of my upbringing, constantly enriched by Christians of other traditions, and by people of other and, very often, of no faith. Perhaps my own experiences of exclusion have helped me to reconsider where the boundaries of God's kingdom might lie. I'd like to think so. Presiding at the Eucharist is both the terrible responsibility and the pure gift that underpins all of the rest of my work as a priest, and yet I know from those old-fashioned Anglo-Catholic priests of my childhood that the 'person' at the centre is Christ, not me. Still a Catholic Anglican, but no longer needing to believe that it is 'best section of the best branch', rather that it is, quite simply, where I have been called to be and to serve and, it would appear, to stay.

*   *   *

Judith Maltby is chaplain and fellow of Corpus Christi College, Oxford, a post she has held since 1993. She earned her doctorate from Cambridge where she was also a research fellow in history at Newnham College. Prior to her present post, she worked in theological education at Wesley College, Bristol, at Salisbury and Wells Theological College and was ordained deacon in the diocese of Salisbury in 1992, and priest in Oxford diocese in the 'first wave' of 1994. Judith is the author and editor of books and articles on the Church of England in the century after the Reformation, including *Prayer Book and People in the Elizabethan and Early Stuart England* (Cambridge University Press, 1998, pbk 2000).

Breaking Down Walls

PHILIPPA BOARDMAN

'It's as if you've got your arms outstretched, saying, "This is my banquet, this is my table, come and share, come and find your own way".' These were the first impressions of one young mum after her early visits to our church. She had come reluctantly, solely to support her nine-year-old daughter who was enquiring about baptism, but had found herself, to her surprise, welcomed, intrigued and drawn in, and now several years later, has come to treasure the Christian community of which she has become an integral part.

Her comment has stayed with me, however, and brings me quiet joy. For the vision of an inclusive Church, where all are welcome and all can find their way, was at the heart of my desire to see both men and women ordained in the Church of England. It was that same vision that took me to the steps of Church House, Westminster on 11 November 1992 to stand and pray with hundreds of others as the debate went on inside the Synod chamber. It was that same vision which I began to glimpse as a reality when we heard the archbishop announce the results of the voting. A gentle Taizé chant began to fill the air and total strangers hugged each other in delight!

Sadly my own early experiences of church had not been such inclusive ones. My childhood request to be part of the church choir was met with 'boys only', and each Sunday I recall having to 'run the gauntlet' of walking past that choir towards the all-male personnel at the altar for a blessing. In my 20s, I remember six of us being ordained deacon, three men and three women, in a wonderful service of commitment and thanksgiving. Twelve months on, it was only the three men who were allowed to go forward to be priested.

Yet the struggle for inclusivity is not a new one. Throughout the Gospels we find Jesus berating the Pharisees for fostering a legalistic culture, effectively demarcating who was 'in' and who was 'out'. Similarly, the epistles and Acts of the Apostles show the believers all too ready to slip back into sectarian ways, only to be challenged again and again by the Spirit of God to dismantle the barriers and make room for all.

The Church in first-century Antioch remains an inspiring example. The city itself was the third largest in the known world, with some half a million people sheltering within the safety of the city walls. But within that walled city, there were other walls, ethnic walls, neighbourhood walls, which had a less positive function. For these walls served literally to divide the people from one another – Syrian, Jewish, Latin, Greek and African sections, each with their own homes, markets and customs. But not their own churches!

In the book of Acts we find the Church overcoming these barriers in a radical way, not least in their leadership. In Acts 13 there is the following leadership line-up: Barnabas, from Cyprus, who had sold property to give to the Jerusalem Church; Simeon, possibly a black Ethiopian Jew, given the epithet 'Niger'; Lucius from Cyrene in north Africa, possibly another black man; Manaen, raised in Herod's court, and Saul (then Paul), who needs no introduction as one of the greatest missionary figures of the Christian Church! Here was a Church of remarkable inclusivity – people from different ethnic groups, different social and economic backgrounds, with profoundly different experiences of life. The walls of Antioch, a great world city, had been transcended.

I have served all my ordained ministry in another great world city, London. Like Antioch, it too has its dividing lines, whether based on age, gender, ethnicity, income, sexual orientation, disability or social background. For those in high-powered careers, long working hours mean that they rarely have a chance to meet their neighbour. Indeed, some see the East End where I live and work, simply as a place to sleep Monday to Friday before retreating to a country home at the weekend. There are barriers of fear, especially for older people going out at night. There are barriers of suspicion towards those of different backgrounds, and there are physical barriers too, whether it be the 'gated entrances' of the privately owned housing developments or the security doors of the council blocks.

It is in this context that the local parish church has a prophetic role to play as a place where all can gather from across the community, to celebrate God's love and to find forgiveness and strength for the hard work of learning to live together with all our differences, hopes and needs. As we meet Sunday by Sunday, I rejoice to minister to and to receive the ministry of a remarkably diverse group of people who not only enjoy fellowship with one another but are active in making a difference in the community. In the spirit of Antioch, our Parochial Church Council includes people from four continents, school-leavers at 15 and those with several degrees, leaders in their fields of paid employment and those who are full time at home with children, someone who is registered disabled, people who might 'label' themselves evangelical, charismatic, liberal and Anglo-Catholic, those who are married, divorced, on their own, with a partner, those who have served in many churches and those for whom our church is just the beginning.

The Bible records that it was in Antioch that the believers were first called 'Christians'. It is not clear exactly how this came about. Perhaps it was inspired by the radical inclusivity of the believers that pointed their fellow citizens beyond human personalities to the One who lived and died and rose again to call all people to himself and the ways of his kingdom. If the legacy of the first ten years of ordained women in the Church of England is that we have progressed a little in this direction, then the struggles are certainly worth it.

* * *

Philippa Boardman was ordained deacon in 1990 and was among the first women to be priested in the diocese of London at St Paul's Cathedral in 1994. She is firmly committed to the parochial system and maintaining a Christian presence in every part of our nation. She has served all her ministry in three inner London parishes in the Boroughs of Waltham Forest, Hackney and Tower Hamlets. She is a member of General Synod and a prebendary of St Paul's Cathedral.

The Table of God's Generosity

FLORA WINFIELD

A Certain Priest, Observed

How does your black waistcoat
button me out of the Church?
Each button to be unfastened
before I can creep in through a button-hole
And hide in your handkerchief pocket.

You fear me, and fasten yourself
neatly, tightly, up to the neck
So that I will not be your undoing.

But I do not want you to give me
your beautiful black buttons
your black waistcoat that secures and binds.

All I ask is to sit
at the table of God's generosity
and know myself at home.

Perhaps, when I can do this, you
will yourself undo
All those little, black buttons.

(Milton Keynes, 1989)

I was the little girl who was never chosen for anyone's team. Sitting with my book in a corner of the garden at school, my greatest wish was to avoid attention, and therefore avoid being bullied. I always felt different – not different as in special, remarkable or unique but different as in out of tune. My father left my mother when I was very small. I can never remember him living at home, although he visited in a casual, charming and unreliable way throughout my childhood. The experience broke my mother, a woman of incredible bravery and humour, who bent in private under a load of sudden bereavement, while sustaining a beautiful performance in public. Like many small children who carry adult loads, I found I had little in common with those of my own age. I was oddly tough, but also oddly vulnerable – perhaps I was just odd. Looking back, I can quite see why no sensible nine-year-old would have chosen my company.

It was in this desperate experience of loneliness and alienation that my sense of vocation began. In the middle of a routine task, thinking of nothing in particular, and seated alone in the late afternoon sunshine, I was suddenly possessed of an overwhelming sense of love, poured out and running over. It was like warm honey flowing though me, like nothing else I could describe or have ever known. Still now, almost 30 years later, I smile as I think of it. Then, in my teens, as life improved and I found ways of no longer being always on the margin, I was sitting alone in a train one evening, coming into a large town at dusk. Looking at the lights I saw thousands of households, each with their own lives and concerns, secrets, agonies and delights; I knew how much pain could be hidden behind bright lights, and I felt that this understanding was somehow required of me, in ways which I did not understand. Through all this, I was sustained by a peaceable and rather undemanding parish church and by school religion – but I could never have spoken of any of this experience of God, illuminating with a peculiar, generous love my fears of abandonment, my sense of difference, my knowledge of myself as an unlikable person.

For me, the experience of vocation has been about weakness – and it has always felt as if that which is most broken in me is that which is most called. And what is called is not only what is saved from the wreckage, what survives and flourishes and grows towards the light, but what remains broken, is unmendable, but is most profoundly touched by God. I found that the place to which I could bring this brokenness was the table where bread, Christ's body, is broken. I came to know the table as a place of reconciliation and restoration, a place of healing and also of belonging and of justice, where there is a space for everyone, and enough for all to eat and be satisfied.

When I came to offer myself to the Church of England, I learnt, painfully, that this kind of self-understanding was best kept quiet. I remember listening to a male contemporary expressing his doubts about his vocation, in a sincere struggle, and thinking, rather ungenerously, that those kind of doubts were a luxury I could not afford, because certainty was always required of us, because we were always making a case for our own existence. In my work as a historian, I researched the history of women in religious orders and in the deaconess movement, and found courage and strength in knowing that I had a history, that other women had passed this way before.

As a parish deacon I worked in Milton Keynes in a Local Ecumenical Partnership, where the church brought together people from a very wide variety of traditions and backgrounds. Each week I set the table for holy communion, led the first part of the service and then stepped back for another minister to preside. Through this experience I came to know two things for which I am grateful – that the real problem which this situation produced was not my problem, which was not being able to preside, but the problem of the people, who felt that when I did not preside they did not celebrate. And I learnt that priestly orders are conferred by the bishop, but that priesthood is also something called out of you by peoples' need.

As a deacon I felt an ambivalence about the Eucharist which has not been entirely resolved by my own ordination to the priesthood. The table, this place of healing and sustaining, where human community could be illuminated and transformed, is also the place which expresses most sharply our divisions as churches. Here is the feast, set on the table of God's generosity, at which God is both host and meal. The feast to which we must invite all who are broken and marginalized, and we are still serving this feast on broken tables.

Lately, I have been writing on Christian anthropology, for a World Council of Churches study. This work has made me turn to questions of the nature of humanity and vocation which I have not thought about for years. I have realized again the importance of understanding our vocations, which are all so personal, so particular, within the greater vocation of the Church. We asked that our vocations might be tested, but in ordaining us the Church of England was also responding to its ecumenical calling. If this vocation to unity is understood not only as the healing of divisions between Christian churches, but as the healing of divisions within the *oikumene*, the whole created order, then being willing to test women's vocations alongside those of men offers the Church a new potential for understanding and healing the most ancient and fearful division, that which denies our common humanity, as women and men made in the image of God.

Of What Are we Made?

We are made of the stars
of dust and soil
Of the longing to bury your feet and stay
knowing a familiar place and faces.

We are made of others' love for us
of their eyes' insight
Of all that we have seen and said
travelled and looked away from.

We are made of all that we have refused and repented
of understanding and ignorance
We make maps of our regrets
the things we are unable to bury
but can't quite bring ourselves
to dig up.

We *are* made of the stars.

(Jerusalem, February 2002)

*   *   *

Flora Winfield has worked in parish ministry in two Local Ecumenical Partnerships and was the first County Ecumenical Officer for Gloucestershire. As chaplain to Mansfield College, Oxford, she was also a member of the university faculty of theology where she taught church history and ecumenics. She worked for five years for the Council for Christian Unity at Church House, Westminster. The author of several books on ecumenism, she is now canon pastor of Winchester Cathedral. Flora has been married for 17 years to Jonathan Gough, a priest.

The poem 'A Certain Priest, Observed' was first published in *Dancing on Mountains: An Anthology of Women's Spiritual Writings*, ed. Kathy Keay and Rowena Edlin-White (HarperCollins 1996).

Unlearning and Relearning Leadership

JANET FIFE

July 1988, a year after my ordination to the diaconate. I am bishop's chaplain while the men I was deaconed with are ordained priest. They are good men, friends. We have shared much. But their calling is being completed while I am a silent spectator, merely a movable stand for the bishop's crook and service booklet. I think of taking the crozier and swinging it about my head; of prelate, provost and priests toppling like ninepins. I remain silent, respectful, contained.

Looking back, a lot of silence seems to have been required of me as a deacon. Which was a pity, since I was not very good at it. During the selection process my call to the priesthood was acknowledged openly, and I was assessed for leadership qualities. At theological college we had all, men and women, been trained for leadership. We debated theology and practice endlessly, and were encouraged to argue strongly. Like the men I took my turn as 'bishop' of various teams. But as a parish deacon I was seldom expected to have ideas of my own, much less to be able to argue a point. Nor did my colleagues expect their own ideas to be debated. In my first three posts I had male colleagues who made decisions regarding our shared ministry without consulting me. They were affronted when these decisions were questioned. Sometimes even the attempt to discuss how these decisions could be worked out in practice seemed to be threatening.

In my first curacy I was not expected to have a public role. My job as a cathedral chaplain was to pastor the congregation. Though this was often rewarding it was also mostly invisible. Despite working 80-hour weeks I was often criticized for laziness. I found, too, that it is difficult to pastor a congregation when you have no say in deciding the preaching programme. Pastoring and teaching go together.

My second curacy was in a large charismatic church where again I was part of a clergy team. I was the first ordained person in that church not to be an elder – though when they came to draft their mission statement they found they needed my skills! When I did finally become an elder my contributions were frequently passed over as if no one had spoken. I began to wonder if I were encased in soundproof glass. There were many complaints about my wearing a clerical collar – though no one seemed to mind my male colleagues wearing theirs. I stopped wearing the collar weekdays but continued to wear it on Sundays. Finally two senior laymen yanked the plastic strip out of my shirt. They were good men who did not mean to be unkind, but it was symptomatic of the Church's problem with women in leadership.

No wonder, then, that when I saw a job advertised where 'visibility' was required, I applied at once. And so I became a university chaplain. Here my gender was no hindrance, except to some of my ecumenical colleagues. The debate about the priesting of women was then at its most intense and sometimes vicious. Like many female deacons I often felt unwanted by my own Church. In universities subversion is valued, however, so this simply gave me added street cred. I took to chaplaincy like a swift to the summer breeze.

Most modern universities have a secular charter, and religion can have no officially recognized place. Chaplains work on the margins and make their own role. They seldom lead from the front; their place is alongside. Many clergy, used to being at the centre of a parish, find this difficult. Having had their own 'territory', it is hard to occupy a tenuous position in someone else's.

For me it was an enormous relief. At last being on the edge was creative rather than destructive. My sense of alienation from the Church I was trying so hard to serve gave me an empathy with people who found the Church strange and unapproachable. I developed a theology of ministry based on being on the margin and without power. Indeed this is essential for mission and for prophetic ministry – but it does not come easily to an established Church. If we are to be a missionary Church in a postmodern society we will need to let go of our power and learn to live effectively on the margins. That's where the love of God meets the need of the world.

So I believe. But that belief did not always serve me well when I returned to parish ministry, this time as vicar. A more upfront style of leadership was required. It was some time before it dawned on me that I was having to unlearn the hard lessons I had learned as a deacon. My leadership qualities had been the source of so much trouble and conflict over the years that I had become afraid of them and was denying them. I have come – painfully! – to realize that I can now acknowledge my strength as a leader. I can accept that it is not a bad thing to have power, but that it needs to be used with wisdom and self-giving love.

Long ago I learned to find God in my experience of being silenced and of rejection. For me the most meaningful day in the church year was Good Friday. Now I am learning to find God in the experience of being heard and respected. This may well carry its own spiritual dangers. But perhaps it is no coincidence that I now lead the Church of the Resurrection.

I would like to conclude with a blessing by Jan Sutch Pickard. This is what I would wish for myself and for all women who lead:

May you stand firm –
yet not be a stumbling block.

May you be open to others –
yet not hollow yourself out.

May you never lose your edge –
yet remember where life's tides
have shaped and smoothed you.

*   *   *

Janet Fife was born in Winchester but grew up in the United States, returning to England in 1974. After gaining an honours degree in English literature at Sussex University she worked in publishing and bookselling before being ordained deacon at the age of 33. She comes from a clergy family and is the sixth to be ordained. Her book *To Be Honest* was published by Daybreak in 1993, and she has researched an MPhil. in the pastoral care of sexual abuse survivors. She is now vicar of the Church of the Resurrection, Upton Priory in Macclesfield. Her two Bedlington terriers keep her earthed.

Visibly Vulnerable

FRANCESCA DIXON

I remember the months before and after the General Synod vote to ordain women to the priesthood as overshadowed for me by a sense of foreboding. A negative vote would have been deeply painful, but in some ways easier, I felt, than a positive one in which we would be asked to break a taboo and to walk through a gateway which had opened only very reluctantly, with many standing aloof, watching us with grim faces. I was grateful to be, by then, well-established in the ministry of a loving congregation, but it was still difficult, in the days after the vote, to have a range of opinions freely voiced by many of them for the first time, and suddenly to feel acutely exposed to possible rejection in a new ministry. It was even more poignant, on the day after the vote, to visit a vicar whom I had never met before, in support of his ministry, and to hear him introduce me to a family in his parish as 'one of those women who are splitting the Church of England'! In common with many other women in this situation, I found the charge that we were agents of divisiveness especially hurtful as it touched a deeply feminine aspiration to nurture and heal.

At that time, the great joy of presiding at the Eucharist was mixed with anxiety about how far I could express myself as a woman in this new role and still be accepted and acceptable. I felt exposed to scrutiny, not just in my performance of priestly liturgical function, but also in my sexual identity, and I found it hard to dismiss from my awareness how negative, and even destructive, my new ministry might be felt to be – particularly in the face of the extreme comments recorded in the press and the instant withdrawal of some male clergy from my deanery chapter. This meant that I never presided at the Eucharist without a sense of spiritual and emotional strain – a feeling which persisted for some years.

I also became aware that this ground-breaking change was presenting a profound challenge to male clergy who might see themselves as in favour of women priests but who had been trained in a style of ministry which was more hierarchical than collaborative. For them, to be confronted with a woman priest was also, I felt, to be confronted in a new way with the otherness of the feminine within themselves and to be challenged to work together interdependently to reveal the complementary nature of male and female. As a woman, I also felt that my approach to pastoral issues tended to put a new emphasis on interconnectedness and the relationship of the emotional to the spiritual. I found it a costly experience to take responsibility for trying to witness to a new, distinctive style of ministry while, at the same time, trying to help others to find this acceptable.

Within a year of my priesting, I left the parish where I had been deaconess and deacon for many years, and I then had an increasingly acute sense of a bewildering paradox: warm acceptance of my ministry and, equally warm rejection – simultaneously. Also, I knew that nothing I could do would lessen the rejection, and that, although some said that it was not intended to be personal, I was unavoidably experiencing it as such. I struggled to know how best to channel the feelings within me of anger and frustration and to find a way of loving in Christ those who had rejected me. I came to see that God was asking me to accept the rejection as a way of sharing, in a very small way, in the suffering of Christ and, from then on, I had a deep sense of being called to be visibly vulnerable as a woman priest – in Christ, and for his sake.

This felt like consenting to having the layers of my skin stripped away like an onion, but I noticed that, in pastoral ministry, I was able to draw closer to others who had been similarly 'stripped' by some personal suffering. Identity, both visible and invisible, has been a persistent issue for me over these years. A vicar, committed to supporting the priestly ministry of women, clearly felt discomfort when seeing me preside at the Eucharist for the first time in his vestments. As I tried later to encourage him to express how he had felt, he suddenly burst out, with a smile, 'It's extraordinary to see you wearing my clothes'!

On the day the first women were ordained to the priesthood in the Church of England (12 March 1994), *The Times*' editorial said, 'Today . . . should be seen as a healing of wounds' – a healing of past injustice and hurt. But Christian healing can only come through the cross, and it seems to me that women priests have been called to be at the centre of a cross-shaped journey which has become more starkly visible in the Church of England in the last ten years. The cross always tests our integrity at an individual and at a corporate level, as the gospel witness to Christ's passion reveals. In this testing, I have felt a great deal of perplexity and inner struggle, but I have tried to hold firm within the light of Christ, praying that I might somehow be enabled to be a hidden channel of his love, especially for those who have rejected me.

The image of the joy and pain of childbirth has been used frequently to describe this upheaval in the Church. Recently, I have had a sense that to be vulnerable and powerless for Christ's sake may be more fruitful than it appears. I now feel that I have more inner freedom and strength to choose that identity, and also that, in a mysterious way, my present position on the margin of the Church may be able to witness to others a little of Christ's suffering and rejected love.

*   *   *

After teaching English and working in the education department of a missionary society, Francesca Dixon trained for ordained ministry at the ecumenical college, Queen's Birmingham. Made a deaconess in 1984, she remained in parish ministry at All Saints', West Bromwich (Lichfield diocese) while she was deaconed in May 1987 and priested in April 1994. In 1995 she was chaplain at Burrswood Christian medical centre. Francesca adds: 'While caring for my husband in his last illness in 1996, I assisted at the Acorn Christian Foundation. In July 1996 we moved to Chichester diocese where I obtained a licence of permission to officiate. My husband died that autumn and, since then, I have assisted and given locum support in the few local village churches open to the priestly ministry of women.'

Costly Creativity

JANE TILLIER

'Come, Holy Ghost, our souls inspire . . .'. As I knelt singing those words at my ordination to the priesthood in a packed Sheffield Cathedral in March 1994, in my heart I was somewhere else entirely. I was lying flat on the floor of the oratory in the home of Una Kroll, veteran campaigner for women's ordination and, at that stage, a deacon in the Church in Wales. I had known that there would not be an opportunity for a full prostration during the service but it was something I felt I needed to do, marking by a physical gesture my self-offering and utter dependence on God. I'd agreed with Una that I would do it as the culmination of the individual retreat that I was making a couple of weeks or so before the ordination. The one moment (in the cathedral) was intimately tied to the other (in the oratory), and I was profoundly moved. I shall never forget the prayers that Una and I offered over my still, vulnerable body as she linked my joy with the costly suffering of many who had gone before. We remembered those who had fought and prayed for the possibility of women priests through many decades. We named particularly those who had died without seeing their hopes realized and those whose lives had been broken in so many different ways by the costly struggle involved. Somehow, through Una's intimate involvement with this issue over many years, I (30 years her junior but to be ordained priest before her as the Church in Wales was yet to vote) carried the hidden cost within me even as I wept tears of joy at the Church's recognition of what I felt I was born to be.

The journey from the steps of Church House in 1992, where I listened anxiously to the debate all day with friends, to my current post as vicar of two parishes in Lichfield diocese has been both immensely rewarding and personally costly. As I write I am struggling with the difficulty of how best to incorporate the second parish which I was asked to take on earlier this year. At the same time I am trying to negotiate some kind of part-time working arrangement so that I can have more time with our toddler and make space for conceiving and carrying a second child. This latter is all the more important in the light of my history of six miscarriages, three before Clare's birth and three since. My area bishop is being very supportive but we are both painfully aware of how difficult it feels to come up with a creative solution in the light of the realities of the financial cost to the Church of tied housing and my being an incumbent rather than a curate, assistant minister or team vicar. We're also sure that this is not just my story but that many women priests of child-bearing age or with young children must be facing difficult decisions in this area which the Church has not wrestled with before. It's a story echoed in many other male-dominated professions as well.

My personal journey over these last ten years has informed my priestly ministry in creative ways that I couldn't have foreseen. Two pictures illustrate how this has been true. The first is set in the local maternity hospital. I am heavily pregnant and a parishioner has just laboured to deliver the stillborn child that she knows has died in her womb. She asks me to hold the baby and to say prayers. A week later I conduct a simple funeral service for the little girl. Her parents explain that they feel able to ask me to do all this, even mindful of my rounded belly, because they know my story of repeated miscarriage. The second picture is set in the church vestry. Three years ago I started a 'Tots' Church' on a Thursday afternoon. Consisting of play, drinks and biscuits, chat and a five-minute offering of music and prayer, it has been a special place of encounter. Three older members of the church, including a widow in her 80s, provide the drinks and the practical support of extra pairs of hands to hold babies. A number of women bring their children faithfully week by week before and after baptism. Sometimes a dad or a granny comes along. The local health visitor recommends the group to new mums. Much of the chat is about pregnancy, labour, baby care, toddler tantrums, potty training and the like, and I join in on equal terms. The creative touch of the living God in so many of these encounters is almost tangible.

I want to end with a prayer that I wrote while on retreat in

May 2000. I was eight months pregnant; the retreat, led by Trevor Dennis, was entitled 'The Midwife God'. Everyone at Chester Retreat House was worried that I would be taking them literally! In the context of this particular book the prayer seems to speak of more than simply my personal experiences of priesthood, miscarriage and birth; it says something about the bumpy journey towards the full integration of women into the priesthood.

A Prayer of Lament to the Midwife God (Psalm 22:9–10)

I no longer want to call you 'Lord'.
We used to get on fine like that;
now it simply will not do!

Three times we lost the seed of life,
the fruit of love and prayer.
Did you hold them in the darkness?
Did you take them to yourself
before the bloody waste was scraped away?

Some wanted me to rail at you,
others wondered how I still could trust;
the worst were those who said you'd done it for the best.
No. I refuse to believe that you would lord it over us like that.

Your touch was so soft and tender
we hardly knew you were there.
You sat on the ground with us whilst we wept.
Somehow you helped us see
that with you no life or love – even the smallest seed
is ever wasted.

Gently I lean on you
and let you snuggle closer.
You're getting back under my skin.

Each wriggle and squirm breeds hope and joy,
with a little fear not far behind.

Can we trust you to bring this life to fruition,
to midwife this life to the light of day?
Who knows?
I simply call down your blessing
on each fruit of my womb.

But I no longer want to call you 'Lord'.

O gentle, tender one
I feel I know you better than before.
I feel I know anew your resurrection peace,
complete with the marks of the nails.
Loss and hope are met together.
Sorrow and joy have kissed each other.

O merciful, hopeful one
hold us gently in your love
and stay with us through what will be. Amen.

*   *   *

Currently vicar of two parishes in North Staffordshire, Jane
Tillier previously served on the staff of Gloucester Cathedral,
following a curacy in Sheffield. Before training for ordination at
Ripon College, Cuddesdon, Jane was lay chaplain at Jesus
College, Cambridge, where she also taught Spanish in the university after completing a doctorate on late-medieval Spanish
poetry. She is married and has one daughter, Clare.

Motherhood and Priesthood: Integrating Roles

GULNAR FRANCIS-DEHQANI

If I were to try to sum up in one word the essence of what the early years of priesthood have been about for me, it would be 'integration'. My interest in the concept of integration began as a personal impulse, gradually taking on wider implications. I now sense the potential towards greater integration – the combining of diverse facets, elements and experiences – not only within myself, but others also. I have a slowly crystallizing vision of how priests may play a part as enablers of this process, first for themselves, then for others and eventually for the whole Church and the world, and in the interplay that exists between these. This, I define as a search towards wholeness, reconciliation, acceptance and integration before God.

I am among the younger generation of women priests. I did not experience the long and painful struggles through years of a God-given calling denied fulfilment by the Church. Instead, my travels took a different route. It was the experience of infertility, the longing for motherhood, the years of invasive and unsuccessful treatment that brought me ultimately to priesthood. Through a personal and agonizing darkness I searched to discover what I should do with the rest of my life, hoping that whatever it was would bring contentment. Eventually I found myself drawn towards ordination.

Following three years' training and after one year as a deacon, I was ordained priest during Michaelmas 1999. At the time I was also ten weeks pregnant. What was to have been one final IVF attempt during the summer before had proved successful. Medical science, nature and God's grace had combined to bring me, at the point of priesthood, to a place of fulfilled contentment.

Our son, Gabriel Iraj, was born in April 2000 and joy untold

paved the way for a gradual realization that from now two vocations – motherhood and priesthood – would need to co-exist, to
be integrated. I could not ignore my priesthood and immerse
myself in being a mother, the very thing I had longed for above
all else. The road to priesthood had transformed me and now
compelled me to continue. Something within me, and beyond,
drew me towards itself. It would have been simpler, certainly in
practical terms, to opt out of stipendiary ministry at least for
several years – to indulge my joy of dreams fulfilled – yet at the
time I felt this was not the right option for me.

My solution was to explore a change in direction by returning
to my curacy on a part-time basis. This was an attempt to enjoy,
in the fullest way possible, the private and public side of my life,
without constant feelings of guilt about doing neither well
enough. There are still in the Church relatively few women in this
situation and each will find solutions of their own. But for the
time being there are not many role models, tried and tested meth-
ods, providing hints at what may work best for all concerned.

Perhaps unsurprisingly then, the responses to my choices from
within church circles have been varied. Most have rejoiced with
me, recognizing that my changed circumstances have opened up
a new dimension for my ministry. They have encouraged me to
explore new ways of being a priest and to regard this as a positive venture, full of unknown opportunities for me and the wider
Church. Others have been delighted to see a variety of human
experiences represented in the ordained priesthood. It has made
the Church seem more real and relevant. A few, however, have
been much more cautious. I have sensed a concern, even fear,
that such expressions of new ministerial models, with the need
for careful management of time and a greater integration of the
personal and professional aspects of life, undermine or threaten
the role of the Church in society. How can a priest truly serve her
community unless she is totally immersed in it and identified
with it? Moreover, at times it has felt like the new model I am
exploring has been regarded as a kind of judgement against those
who operate within the more traditional patterns. It need not,
however, be so.

So for me the journey continues. Not to demarcate with precise accuracy the roles of mother and priest, but to learn how
fully to integrate the two. There are, of course, always time limi-

tations and practical considerations, but both motherhood and priesthood are about more than doing a particular job, in a given time, before clocking off. They are for me about learning to 'be'. Existing before God by striving to fulfil my potential in any given situation and allowing myself to give of my best. Permitting the different elements of the two vocations to co-exist, to merge and feed each other.

My experiences have been deeply personal, yet they have led me to reflect on the potential for greater integration in other aspects of our lives. I see the potential for fewer defined boundaries around the components that make us who we are, at least psychologically and emotionally. I recognize that the Church, while separate from the world, must also be integrated into the world. As priests and lay people, we must move comfortably and unhindered between the two if we are to witness God's presence in both.

My adventures into priesthood and motherhood have only just begun. I hope that for myself and my family, and together with the whole of God's Church, we can move forward to recognize the changes represented by alternative models of ministry as positive and life-giving, something that needs to be loved, nurtured and encouraged if it is to bear fruit. And yes, I am hopeful about the future.

*   *   *

Gulnar (Guli) Francis-Dehqani was born in 1966 in Iran. She moved to England after the 1980 Islamic Revolution and has, to date, been unable to return to Iran. A Nottingham University music graduate, she worked at BBC World Service and domestic radio's religious department. Her PhD from Bristol University was awarded in 1999 soon after she was ordained. Formerly a curate in Mortlake with East Sheen, she is now chaplain to the Royal Academy of Music and St Marylebone Church of England Secondary School. Guli and her husband Lee, also ordained, live in Richmond, with their two-year-old son.

Questioning Stereotypes of Sexuality and Gender

HELEN DUCKETT

I had only been in my current post as team vicar for two months when I discovered I was pregnant with my first child. Although my husband (who is also a team vicar but in a different parish) and I were overjoyed, and could ourselves see no reason why we could not successfully combine parenthood with our respective parochial ministries, there was, nevertheless, on my part, considerable apprehension as to how my congregation and those in the wider community would respond to our news. Besides having recently arrived, I would soon be taking at least six months maternity leave from a church which had just experienced a two-and-a-half year interregnum. Women priests might be a relatively new phenomenon in the Church of England, but pregnant women priests are an even greater rarity. 'Would my congregation', I asked myself, 'now regret the fact that they had chosen a young woman as incumbent – a woman who didn't want to be only a vicar but also a mother?' Would I also be reconfirming any sexist stereotypes that might have been held about women being unreliable workers because they always have to keep taking time off for 'family matters'?

Of course, the fact that I was even thinking such things is telling in itself – especially as such concerns were not even crossing my husband's mind in respect of his congregation. However, although I was anxious, I have to say that when I told them my news, and reassured them that I was planning to come back to work full time after the baby had been born, my parishioners were amazingly generous, enthusiastic and overwhelmingly positive in their response. We were snowed-under by presents of knitted cardigans, blankets, booties and Mothercare vouchers; and these were given not just by the core congregation but by people on the fringes of the church as well – people whose baptisms, weddings and relatives' funerals I had taken. They included the children and staff in the local schools; the Neighbourhood Watch and local tenants and residents groups and the senior citizens clubs. For all these folk, and for others, the fact that I was a priest and was pregnant was very definitely a good thing; and according to them, the main reason it was a good thing was that in their eyes it made me, their vicar, seem more 'human', more 'accessible', more 'real'. In the past, my parishioners would tell me, male priests would often come across as being 'remote', 'distanced', slightly 'stand-offish'- removed from 'everyday' people's lives, and rather too fond of academic, long-winded and unintelligible pronouncements from the pulpit! But with women priests, and especially with expectant women priests, this perceived gap between laity and clergy was now being bridged. Apparently, not only were female vicars 'easier to talk to' and were 'naturally' more 'caring', 'sympathetic' and 'pastoral', pregnant women vicars, like me, were even more 'down-to-earth'. Sharing the common female experience of child-bearing and child-birth helped to remove them from their spiritual priestly pedestal, and put them on an equal footing with 'normal' women.

Such responses obviously raise huge questions about the stereotypes and expectations that surround issues of gender and sexuality, and understandings of the identities and roles of women and men both in the Church and in the wider world. Many male vicars are incredibly pastorally sensitive and caring, so why have male priests in the past been perceived as remote and inaccessible? Many male vicars have children, so why is the pregnancy of a female vicar deemed as being so significant?

And what if I, as a woman priest, was married, but had no intention of having children – would I seem so 'normal' and 'down-to-earth' then? Have people responded so well to my pregnancy because I am upholding for them the patriarchal ideal that a woman's role and true fulfilment in life can ultimately only be found not in her work, but in motherhood?

While noting these reservations, there has still been for me something incredibly profound about the way my parishioners have responded to my pregnancy, and to my daughter as well, now that she has been born. Towards the end of my nine months and when my bump was so big that it was clearly visible even beneath a chasuble and alb(!), people would often relate how moving and challenging it was for them to have me preside at communion, or conduct a baptism or funeral. Because in an institution where, rightly or wrongly, much is often symbolically located in the priest/vicar, somehow the presence of a heavily pregnant body behind the altar, or in the pulpit, or next to the font – a body that was obviously physically straining and vulnerable – was for my congregations a very real image for them of what they hoped and desired the Church to be. That is, a Church where the presence of God is acknowledged and named in *all* aspects of life – even in the physical, passionate and emotional experiences of sex and labour, and in all the messiness that comes with it: blood and semen and ovulation and stitches and stretch-marks and epidurals and episiotomies, and the almost primeval pain and terror, exhilaration and relief. Not only is God's presence to be found in these things, my being pregnant and being a priest was also for my parishioners an affirmation that their 'normal' and 'everyday' lives are so diffused and transfused by God that they themselves are sacred, are holy.

Such an affirmation and awareness should not, of course, be new – for what other belief should lie at the heart of a faith which confesses that God was incarnate in human flesh and human experience? But if my ministry as a vicar, and my particular personal circumstances, have subverted just one person's misunderstanding and misconception of the Church, and have enabled just one person to realize in a new and different way that God is truly present in and with them, then for myself there is even more reason to give thanks to my Creator for calling me to be both a priest and a mother.

*   *   *

Helen is currently working in her first incumbent's post as team vicar of the Church of SS Augustine and Chad in Wednesfield, Wolverhampton, and lives in Walsall where her husband, Keith, is also a parish priest. She has studied theology at undergraduate and post-graduate level at Oxford, Sheffield and Birmingham universities. She trained for the priesthood at Queen's College, Birmingham, and was ordained deacon in 1998 and priest in 1999, while serving her curacy in Cannock in the Lichfield diocese.

What Should I Call You?

JANE HASLAM

Two call me 'mummy'. I change nappies and I mop up tears. I treasure crayon drawings and playdough animals. I find lost socks, lost mittens, lost shoes, lost anything. I provide lunch and tea with lots in between (daddy does breakfast). I teach manners and control tantrums. I teach road safety and set limits. I push swings and help on slides. I wash clothes and dirty toys. I read books and play favourite videos.

One calls me 'partner'. We share home and daily life. I do the weekly shop and pay the bills. I arrange the insurance policies and do the tax returns. I book our holidays. I walk the dog and feed the cat. I gratefully eat all the meals he cooks for me. We drink wine together. We listen to each other, support each other, offer each other our opinions and advice. We read the papers, listen to the radio and watch television together.

Two call me 'daughter'. I talk regularly on the telephone and provide updates on grandchildren. I send numerous photos of the same as well as many thank you cards for presents received by post. They visit us at Christmas and Easter when I'm working. We visit them in between, when we are not working. I encourage them to babysit for a few hours and sometimes even for whole weekends!

One calls me 'sister'. I'm an infrequent correspondent and less frequent visitor. But I'm there if I'm needed as he is for me. I care quietly and at a distance. Our lives are so very, very different. We communicate mostly via our parents.

Some call me 'friend'. I talk on the telephone. I occasionally manage to visit. Sometimes friends are able to visit us. I celebrate good news and I am sorrowful at the sad and pray. I send gifts and cards for births and birthdays, baptisms and weddings and sometimes for no reason at all.

Some call me 'neighbour'. I chat over the fence, by the post box or across the road. I turn off house alarms and I take in the post. I hold spare keys (just in case) and I feed pets during holidays. I seek and share information on local events and issues. I give and receive practical help – sharing baby equipment, household appliances, buckets of water . . . Some evenings I babysit and some I'm a guest at parties.

Some call me 'Reverend' (though thankfully never yet 'Mother'). I baptize children – some while they sleep and some while they struggle. I listen to incredible life stories and take many funerals. I plan services and lead worship with help from eagle-eyed servers. I preach and tell stories about God's infinite love and longing for all people. I lead Bible studies and hope that in them we encourage each other's faith. I visit those who are sick or simply overwhelmed. I enjoy passing on 'good news' through the parish magazine and other publicity. I photocopy and give lifts. I organize games. I support my colleagues in their many responsibilities and benefit in turn from their support. I rejoice with people and I grieve with them.

What should you call me?

Some still aren't sure.

But my name is Jane and, in everything I am and I do, I am a priest in the Church of God. I am deeply grateful for the privilege.

*   *   *

Jane Haslam was ordained priest at Wells in 1998, minutes before her husband (they met at Trinity College, Bristol). Having just married they chose to serve their title together in the parish of Minehead. Jane and Michael were the first official job-share in the diocese. They both enjoyed working full time until their daughter was born, after which they alternated work and childcare. Michael was then offered a post in Newcastle and they moved in August 2000. Jane spent a year out during which Adam was born until, in September 2001, she was appointed to a part-time stipendiary assistant post in a church in North Shields.

The Call of the Wider Church: Partnership and Creativity

JACKIE SEARLE

I was among the first priests in the Church of England to give birth, being eight months pregnant when ordained in St Paul's Cathedral. A surplus makes great cover-all maternity wear. On the day of the ordination, waiting in procession, I expressed concern to my neighbour, who had been a midwife (I am sure we had been thoughtfully placed together), that I might get twinges during the service. 'Don't worry,' she replied, 'you're being ordained by someone renowned for his deliverance ministry!'

In the ordination service a speaker was allowed to object. There were attempts to prevent the service going ahead right up to the last minute. When the objector had finished his speech outlining the reasons why, to his mind, the ordination of women as priests was unacceptable, the bishop again put the question 'Is it therefore your will that they should be ordained?' I will always remember the response. The cheering could not be stopped as the congregation shouted very loud, 'IT IS!' The clapping and jubilation filled the cathedral. It was the most moving moment, and one that has sustained me in the years since. I did not make this decision alone to be a priest – this was made with many others and after much testing. The congregation that day, representing the wider Church, promised to uphold us in our ministry. The calling is a daunting one, in a time when the Church is being tested in many ways. I believe that the partnership of women and men and children in the call of God is crucial to the growth of the Church.

So priesthood and parenthood were very intimately combined for the first months after becoming a priest and have continued to be so, but in less intensive ways. In those early months of night-time feeds and general mayhem, I learned much about unconditional love, nurture and patience. My spiritual director encouraged me to think of these two gifts – a baby, and a priestly ministry, as complementary and combined, and so they have been. One of our neighbours, a Catholic, once said he was mystified as to how I could be a priest – married, female and with children – how could I focus on the things of God? At times I think he's got a point! But I believe that the incarnation shows us God in the middle of family life, of human relating, of home and community. There are times when I go with the children to school, they speed along on their scooters, and I trot along behind with lunch boxes and book bags thinking, 'The Christian Priest Today'.

My current environment is a theological college – the optimistic end of the Church of England. It is full of enthusiastic and faithful people training together for ministry. Some of the women now in training were still at school in November 1992. The door to ordination is wide open for them, and sometimes learning about the Act of Synod and its repercussions comes as a shock. The impression from the training perspective is that all sorts of women, from all stages of life, are being recommended for ministry, but finding positions that are right for them is not always easy. In particular, those with children, or with special reasons for needing to be in a particular area, find that few dioceses think creatively and flexibly about working patterns. My expectation is that this will change as the dioceses which do offer good practice and model a creative approach to ministry will provide an example which can be followed.

*   *   *

Jackie Searle was ordained to the priesthood in St Paul's Cathedral, London, on 16 April 1994. She was curate at Christ Church, Roxeth, then St Stephen's, Ealing, before becoming tutor in applied theology and Dean of Women at Trinity College, Bristol. She is married to the Revd David Runcorn and has two children, Joshua and Simeon.

Acceptance and Joy

EMMA PERCY

I remember 11 November 1992 as a day of tension and then euphoria; returning to Bedford from London to find a full answering machine and a porch full of flowers and champagne. Then we were told to wait and not to be triumphant. So I waited while getting on with being a deacon in a busy, eucharistic parish.

On 22 September 1993 I became a mother. Ben was born and the church bell ringers rang a quarter peal for the curate's son. I took maternity leave and returned to parish work. On 23 April 1994 I was ordained priest. I was number 60 in a mammoth service at St Albans Abbey where 62 women were ordained. The Abbey was full and crowds waited outside, and somewhere my poor parents-in-law paced with a crying baby wanting a feed from his mother. These last ten years have been for me a period of growing into these two roles, mother and priest, priest and mother. I have added one more son, Joe, and have moved from my training parish to a new university chaplaincy and into my first incumbency.

The most remarkable thing for me is how smoothly it has gone and how accepted I am. Initially there were painful moments when parishioners I had pastored as a deacon stayed away from any service where I presided as a priest. Recently a priest would not allow me to take my nanny's wedding at her home church and only allowed me to participate if I wore 'a flowery dress and no dog collar'. Yet mostly I am struck by how readily accepted I am as a priest by my own congregation and by the wider community. People find me approachable because I'm a mum, I'm like them. When I came on interview to Holy Trinity, PCC members were invited to meet the prospective vicar. They knew nothing and it was a treat watching the faces as they realized that the young woman with the baby was in fact the candidate. One said to the wardens later, 'When we said we didn't mind a woman, we didn't think we'd get one!' Four years on we have all worked together to help this parish to grow and flourish, and they like being the parish with the woman vicar.

My time at Anglia Polytechnic University was a challenging time to work out my sense of being a priest. Only six weeks after my ordination I found myself without a congregation or a church or chapel. I did celebrate the Eucharist in lecture rooms, but it was not the heart of my ministry. What was interesting was how much more confident I was to work in this mission situation representing the Church in a secular institution, now that I felt the Church truly owned and accepted my ministry. I was a priest and that was more than being able to do certain things; it was about being someone who could represent God and the Church to this diverse community. It was a rewarding time, and I am particularly grateful to those who also provided places for me to preside at the Eucharist, especially John Binns at Great St Mary's.

It is so exciting for me that the Church has ordained women when I was still quite young. I am still in my 30s and able to give energetically to the life of the parish, and as a priest I can be in the role of vicar, able to lead the parish. I am able to fulfil the role that I felt God calling me to in my teens, when it had seemed impossible.

As a mother I have found it a wonderful job to combine with bringing up my children. The vicarage is a busy place with children, nanny (now au pair), and parishioners in and out in a wonderful complex partnership. On one occasion my husband said it was like an advent calendar, someone new behind every door! My mothering and my ministry are collaborative and I am able to bring vision, shape and leadership to both roles. The wider Church is still at times a frustratingly masculine place and I long for the insights that women bishops and other senior clergy could bring. I have also come up against nice men who like women – but find they don't know how to treat them as colleagues. There are still cultural shifts that need to be made, but slowly women are beginning to leaven the lump.

All in all my experience is good. I am a fulfilled parish priest struggling with all the issues of parochial ministry. I have a wonderful honorary curate in my husband whose support throughout our 12 years of ministry and 13 years of marriage, has been invaluable. Often I am in the local infant school where the children all know Emma the vicar and it delights me that from an early age their image of a vicar is one that I, at their age, never imagined. What a joy that the Church has changed.

*   *   *

Born Emma Bray in 1963, she was educated at Woodford County High and then read history at Jesus College, Cambridge. After a few years of travel and part-time jobs she studied at Cranmer Hall and gained a degree in theology. In 1989 she married Martyn a fellow ordinand and the following year they were ordained deacon to serve as curates in St Andrew's, Bedford. They moved to Cambridge in 1994, where Emma set up the chaplaincy at the Cambridge campus of Anglia Polytechnic University. At the end of 1997 they moved to Sheffield where Emma is priest in charge of Holy Trinity Millhouses and Martyn runs a theological research institute. She is the mother of Ben (8) and Joe (5).

From Unthinkable to Unremarkable

JANE CHARMAN

I was ordained to the priesthood on my thirty-fourth birthday. 'What a wonderful birthday present for you,' said friends who knew what it meant to me. That's how I remember it, as a day of new birth, not just for me, not just for the capacity congregation which crowded into Ely Cathedral that afternoon, not just for the peculiar institution we call the Church of England, but for the whole Church.

When a baby is born, three things need to happen. First, the parents conceive of the child in their imagination. They picture the child they hope for and eagerly anticipate its arrival. Second, a child must be conceived physically. The idea of a child must be realized in the flesh, embodied. Third, there must be a time of delivery and the parents must receive the child they have brought into being and commit themselves to it for the future. It's a fact of life that few births are accomplished without risk and pain and emotional upheaval, even when the outcome is a joyful one.

As I pass my days happily as a parish priest of three much-loved small rural parishes, I sometimes think of the women who conceived the vision for us at the beginning, waiting, hoping and working for a time when the Church would be able to acknowledge the priestly calling of women as well as men. Many of these women we know by name, through their writings and through the memories we have of them. For some of them the time came too late. Some others were able to minister as priests for a few years only. There is sadness and a sense of waste in this but also a deep sense of indebtedness. These women were bearers of our hope at a time when the burden was a heavy one. They are our godmothers in ministry and for that we thank them.

Thinking back to the day on which it all became possible, 11 November 1992, my most vivid memory is of my own feeling of amazement when Archbishop George Carey announced the result of the voting. I remember a slight tremor in his voice as he spoke, but could not tell whether it was an expression of his personal delight or whether he was simply aware that history was about to be made. I was one of those who had not expected a 'Yes' vote, although I had campaigned vigorously for it. I think many people on both sides of the debate had not expected it. My husband and I had already discussed what we would do; we would go abroad, offer ourselves for ministry in a part of the Anglican Communion where we could both be priests. The letters of reference had been written, the job interviews arranged. This single piece of news changed our future, just as the future is changed for ever when a couple first finds out that they are expecting a baby. Our joy was real, but it was mixed with apprehension. We knew that not everything would be easy.

Ten years later we are still living through what has been described as a process of reception, although there is no single agreed definition of what this process is and how it is supposed to work. I count myself fortunate that I have always ministered in settings where there has been majority acceptance of my priesthood. Others have faced much greater challenges and received much less support, some have been treated outrageously. We are still a church without women bishops. In general, though, I believe the climate is now one of growing acceptance. Like most of us, I was the first woman incumbent in the parishes where I now serve. Not everybody was in favour of my appointment and some declared that they would never be able to receive communion from me. In fact almost all now do. Our staff team includes those who have or have had reservations about the priestly ministry of women, but we have found it possible to continue alongside one another. As for the future, let me put it this way: I have met a great many people who used to be opposed to women priests but are now in favour. I have yet to meet anyone for whom the opposite is true.

One of our fixed beliefs about the Church of England is that it handles change badly. I have often thought that we underestimate ourselves. The last decade has been one of far-reaching change which has been handled for the most part with courage, common sense and many shining examples of courtesy, flexibility and faithfulness. Things which would have been unthinkable ten years ago are already becoming unremarkable. In 1997 when I announced that I would be taking maternity leave to have our first baby, I became an agenda item at the next meeting of the Bishop's Council. There was a flurry of media interest. My parishes were first astonished, then apprehensive, and finally rather pleased with their new and daring image. By 2001, when I gave birth to our second daughter, there was an air of quiet routine about the whole thing. It seems to me that the Church of England is already well on the way to integrating, not just the idea, but the reality of the ministry of women priests. The future we prayed for is before us, what we have to do now is live it.

*   *   *

Jane Charman is rector of Duxford and vicar of Hinxton and Ickleton in the diocese of Ely. She was first licensed in 1985 as a stipendiary lay minister in the diocese of Gloucester where she helped to found an action and support group for women wishing to explore their vocation to the priesthood. During 1990–95 she was chaplain of Clare College, Cambridge, ministering as a deacon and involved in campaigning for the ordination of women priests. Her husband Bill is a non-stipendiary priest, and they have two small daughters, Matilda and Trelawny.

Priesthood and Society

WENDY BRACEGIRDLE

It was the morning after the vote in General Synod on the ordination of women to the priesthood. Elated myself, what caught me unprepared was the reaction to that decision by the world beyond the gathered Church. I set off from home to walk the mile through the city streets to the diocesan offices. During the first few hundred yards I began to wonder what it might be about my appearance that was causing the 'beeps' from cars and lorries. (At 40, I was already well-drilled by my daughters that I was far too elderly to expect admiration.) Further up the road, I met a pedestrian, a stranger. He said, 'What a great vote! Congratulations.' A lorry driver slowed and called out of the cab window, 'About time too!' All the way to work that morning I met ordinary people who did not know me personally but saw my dog-collar and wanted to express their welcome for the vote. It was an astonishing display of awareness of the affairs of the Church. The vote was an event noted and celebrated out there on the streets.

It is that acceptance and welcome of the ordination of women by the wider world that has been a constant source of joy, even reassurance, over these first years. In all this time I have not met a single person beyond Church circles who has questioned, rejected or appeared hostile to a woman priest. Only among a very tiny number of church people (none in my home parish) have I met negativity. This surely sets the curious notion of 'reception' in its proper place. Society – the world in which God calls us to be priests – finds itself naturally and whole-heartedly able to receive and to 'own' this ministry. The priesthood that flows from the heart of God, upwelling and inspired by the Spirit, authorized and properly ordered by the Church, is authenticated, recognized and validated by the society of men and women among whom it is exercised. It is not the privatized possession of the organization, but something infinitely broader. Our society, however secularized, still seeks in many and various ways truths and meanings that lie beyond description. In our time, that society has come to welcome women alongside men as interpreters, representatives and guides in the common pilgrimage.

Robert and I were married in September 1973. Two weeks after our wedding, Robert was ordained deacon. When, the following year, he was ordained priest, it was naturally a great joy for both of us, yet there had also entered into our lives a separation that would not be undone until I was priested 20 years later. When both have a strong sense of calling as priests but ordination has been denied to one partner, there is a mysterious sense of incompleteness, something hard to articulate and best not named too often during the waiting. The close of one journey and the beginning of the next happened for me at a very precise moment. At the altar, the first time I presided at the Eucharist, I turned to Robert, standing beside me, to communicate him: 'The body of Christ.' I placed the host in his hands and nearly broke down crying, because at last our marriage was truly consummated.

There remains, I believe, much to explore in the richness of married priesthood, more to be described than a facile, oversimplified thesis of complementarity. Sociologists, psychologists and research students have seized upon ordained couples as a rich, convenient new research topic. But so far they have largely failed to address their subject with any theological creativity.

Meanwhile, many bishops seem mystified by the new phenomenon, ill-equipped to recognize rich potential, readier to anticipate problems and quite unable to understand a couple as one unity yet two persons. (Surely, in a Church of trinitarian and Chalcedonian orthodoxy, we might expect, at the least, an intellectual grasp of this.) We were called with other ordained couples to a meeting with four bishops. The conversation that ensued did not go very deep. It was too soon, and the parameters of the discussion were too narrow, too polite. The bishops seemed dismayed that not all the couples said the daily office together. It was hard to explain that some of us, within such an intimate identity of vocation, require both the sharing of prayer and worship yet also some spiritual space. The very joys of a twin vocation could easily turn into a claustrophobic imprisonment. Perhaps a comparable situation is the need of identical twins to express their individuality.

The marriage of two priests would be easy to overromanticize. I have not yet found clear ways to understand or define the experience, the reality or its significance. We need poets and good theologians to do this, perhaps. All I know is that the truths of it lie in a sacramental theology that embraces the heart of incarnation and transcendence, marriage-bed and altar.

And what of Acts of Synod, PEVs, 'A', 'B' and 'C' and the equivocation of bishops who do know better? Well, we still have a journey to make, requiring the firm tread of truth and the good compass of faith.

Meanwhile, a regular acquaintance, Paul, a down-and-out, huddled within his once-cream blanket on the dusty thoroughfare in Manchester, has a request. A few weeks ago he asked for a Bible. Today he says to me, 'Will you give me a blessing, Father?'

*   *   *

Canon Wendy Bracegirdle has been principal of the Manchester Ordained Local Ministry Scheme since 1989. She has worked in theological education for 28 years, and spent five years in hospital chaplaincy. Her own specialized full-time ministry has been grounded in her participation in the parochial ministry of Robert, her husband. Together they have lived and worked in urban priority areas since 1975, in large council overspill estates in Birkenhead and then in inner-city Salford. A member of the General Synod, Wendy has served on two national working parties concerned with ministry and training.

The Call to Wait

SHEILA WATSON

'Grey hair – it was the grey hair, not the blondes or brunettes, that moved me. I had no idea so many had waited so long.' A friend made this unexpected comment after the first ordination of women to the diaconate in St Paul's Cathedral in March 1987, hitting upon one of the central demands of ordination – the call to wait.

It is a call that asks for perseverance through good and bad, through thick and thin. It might be at a bedside with the dying, or in a cold church when prayer no longer has meaning, or in the interminable struggle for institutional change.

Sometimes, for me, it has featured moments of despair at the unseen pain in so many people's lives, clergy and lay, as well as joy in the celebrations of births and marriages. At other times sheer frustration at the apparent inability of the Church to look beyond its own concerns has made me want to run.

Each time this has happened I have been drawn back by the God who waits so patiently for us in the garden of Gethsemane and in the new life of the resurrection. We are all called to share in the divine waiting. 'The faith and the love and the hope are all in the waiting' as T.S. Eliot tells us.

At the first ordinations to the priesthood in 1994, it was a different kind of grey hair that moved me. As I celebrated the Eucharist for the first time, from the unfamiliar central position behind the altar, I remember looking at the congregation in St Luke's, Chelsea. In front of me were rows of grey heads, my supporters to whom I owed so much.

There was the Roman Catholic Mayor coming forward to receive a blessing, our patron who had made a special journey from his Scottish estate, and the women, even members of the Prayer Book Society, who had lived through the almost forgotten struggles of the twentieth century. There were those who had studied for degrees they had been unable to receive because of their gender, as well as those who knew at first hand the fight for recognition in professions such as medicine. It was a scene that confounded expectation. There are so many unfounded assumptions about ageing congregations, their attitude to women and much more besides, and in questioning these assumptions, the grey hairs captured another call experienced in priesthood – to follow the God of surprises and the unexpected.

Who would expect to find the Most High God in a stable in Bethlehem or on Calvary? Yet this is the God from whom we draw comfort, the God who points us in so many unexpected directions. God might be the God of waiting, but as God of the unexpected, this does not imply a God of inactivity.

When I worked in the selection process, listening to ordinands talking about their sense of vocation, I would often hear women say, 'No, I could not believe God was asking me. I'm not special in any way, not equipped to deal with all the demands and the bits of hostility.' But of course the ordinary and the unlikely are precisely those whom God has always called!

Among those unlikely ones, apart from myself, is the other significant head of grey hair in my life of ministry – my husband. He went grey so early I have never known him as the blonde he once was. Together we have faced the waiting and the unexpected challenges that come from being a couple who are both ordained. We have been lucky in that we've always had complementary posts. We have also, I believe, been accidentally helped by both having been in full-time ministry before we married, being at different ages and stages of the priestly journey as well as, sadly, not having children.

It was never suggested that one of us needed to be non-stipendiary, though there have been precarious moments. I once left one job not knowing what the next would be in our new setting. I know that many couples in this situation have different experiences. With clergy couples on the increase, there is an urgent need to look at what this might be telling us about styles of ministry. The work has begun in a number of places, but it is sometimes forgotten that the Church of England has a monopoly in employing women priests. It can't follow the example of large businesses where employees who marry are often encouraged – if not ordered – to work for different companies.

As we approach the tenth anniversary of the vote, I am glad that there are fewer experiences of the kind I met at the Advisory Board of Ministry in the early 1990s, when too many would assume that, as a woman, I dealt only with women's selection.

When I'm feeling fed up, I still treasure the memory of the unknown man walking down Great Smith Street on the day of the vote in his tweed three-piece suit and brown trilby. As we drew level, he looked up, saw my collar and said 'Hope you win, then!' He too confounded expectation and gave me hope.

The hope persists, even though the grey is now beginning to show on my own head.

*   *   *

Sheila Watson is the archdeacon of Buckingham. She was an honorary canon of Salisbury Cathedral and director for the Diocesan Board of Ministry. Her husband, Derek, was the dean of the Cathedral. First a deaconess in the Episcopal Church in Scotland, she waited eight years before deaconing and a further seven before priesting. Her journey to Salisbury and Buckingham has been via the North East and London, including a spell in adult education in the diocese of London and as senior selection secretary at the Advisory Board of Ministry, Church House Westminster.

Diary Notes and Wry Observations

KATHARINE RUMENS

Saturday morning

I am in the church. I am on duty so I wear a clerical collar, and jeans, because there may be messy jobs to do. Perhaps it is the casual attire or the fact that I am demolishing flower arrangements and sorting out the children's area, at any rate I am rendered virtually a non-person. This is an interesting experience as I usually wear a jacket and skirt, and always black shirts. I think there's no mistaking me, and for City functions I now possess black shirts with tonsure collars: I dress up to the job, though not on Saturday mornings. Today a woman asks me to break down a £10 for her, which was a nuisance – I have to go and rattle around in the flower fund – and she barely thanks me. What do I want apart from thanks? Conversation, or recognition, so that I can modestly inform her I am in charge?

The church bells are rung by visiting bands, ringers start arriving and stand about reading the notice boards. One woman matches the photo of the rector with the woman in jeans. She tells me it is nice to see 'a lady in charge'. I mentally arm myself for the ladyship dialogues which experience has taught me not to engage with unless feeling strong. It goes with those other sub-groups of lady priests and lady vicars, and may deteriorate into what is thought to be the novelty of the priestess/rectress construct. I am sure a supportive member of the congregation would be hurt if I told him I did not find it acceptable to be addressed as rectress even in jest, similarly the friend who made observations about 'priestesses in your coven' on his Christmas card. That's the trouble with female clergy, we have no sense of humour. The bell-ringer asks me if I know another woman priest who is in charge of a collection of villages in the Cotswolds. I don't – there are these assumptions that somehow we do all know each other.

I am proud of our ringers – they have just appointed Gwen as Tower Secretary. She is the first woman in the Ancient Order of College Youths to be elected to this office and only the second woman to be elected an official. The Society held a referendum in 1998 and voted to admit women. (They briefly had women members in the first years of the twentieth century, but kicked them out again in 1919.) Here in the City, which prides itself on (male) traditions, Anne is the Director of Music, and Lesley, the Parish Administrator, is the only woman member of the Company of Parish Clerks, and now we have Gwen.

A colleague has recommended a woman in his congregation to find her way to St Giles. She can no longer bear saying 'for us men and our salvation' in the Creed. It is not the task of a female-led Church to become a women's refuge, but we may find ourselves offering shelter.

Wednesday morning

Straight after morning prayer I get a phone call from the master of a livery company. He congratulates me, my name is to be put forward as the next chaplain. No other names are to be offered, thus I may consider myself chaplain from August. This constitutes a departure from tradition in a company that does not admit women.

The selection process has been a number of conversations, including one with the master and the upper warden. Their big question was would I be able to manage in an all-male environment? Manage what? There have also been invitations to lunch and dine which have felt like auditions, perhaps to discern my social skills in an all-male environment.

I had to say grace at the dinner; the wives of the court were at the reception beforehand, and when dinner was announced they all went to the lodge to eat by themselves, leaving me in the company of the men. The wife of one of the speakers was incensed at being banished; this was a tricky one. Should I enter into her indignation, thereby ruining my chances of being accepted, or be placatory?

Basically, all this can be three hours of being addressed as 'dear', but it is also about being agents of change and equality outside as well as inside the Church. In moderation.

How satisfying to know I have made history this week, and it is still only Wednesday morning.

Wednesday mid-morning

There's a big service at St Paul's. There are different parts of the procession – Philippa is with the prebendaries, Lucy is with the cathedral staff and I am with the City incumbents. On the other hand, the three women representing other Christian traditions are a sizeable percentage of their bit.

It is still a reflex action to count the ordained Anglican women, especially when it can be done on the fingers of one hand in a full cathedral. I observe how few we are to a man I had hitherto thought to be reconstructed: 'Oh really, I didn't notice,' he said.

On another occasion while waiting to process, the man behind me asked the man beside me, 'Who is your lady companion?' I introduced myself as Katharine from St Giles' Cripplegate (the invitation, after all, was to City incumbents). 'And what do you do there?' he asked.

There are issues about the cost of maintaining the visibility of ordained women's ministry, and the necessity of finding a friend to drink Scotch with.

Thursday evening

My name still hasn't been added to the list of incumbents of the parish. There is no more space on the brass plaque dating back to Aylward 1135, so I will appear on the marble one, which begins with William Nichols 1733. I never use my degree – it is a reaction to an environment which bristles with boasted pomp and show. Now that I am to be set in stone, I succumb for posterity.

*   *   *

Katharine Rumens is rector of St Giles' Cripplegate and the first female incumbent in the City of London. Before ordination she was a fashion designer. She trained at Westcott House and was ordained deacon in 1992, priest in 1994. She has worked in the dioceses of Chelmsford and Southwark. St Giles' is in the Barbican and as well as a large residential population, the parish includes the Arts Centre and City institutions.

Becoming a Just Church

NERISSA JONES

A number of us camped outside Lambeth Palace for three days before the vote. It was a vigil of prayer, and of solidarity with the Archbishop of Canterbury, who was in favour of women priests. There was a strange contrast, though, in the way Lambeth regarded us. At the gatehouse, we could not have been more kindly welcomed and looked after by the porter; senior staff going in and out only glanced our way. The archbishop was driven in and out with his face averted.

Even the agnostic public saw the matter as one of justice, of human equality which should be unassailable, particularly to the Church. A Church discriminating has a theological fault line which mocks and endangers its very existence. Embracing injustice with regard to women, somewhere along the line, a church is sitting quite comfortably alongside the Taliban.

But isn't all that over? No. The years since the vote are symbolized for me by the averted face of the archbishop. Yes, he voted for us, but at the same time he could not look at us. Ten years on, the hierarchy of the Church of England keeps its face averted. Women remain an embarrassment which was hustled to one side by the infamous Act of Synod. As time has gone on, individual bishops, I know, much regret that injustice. But it remains.

My own time as a priest has been so free from discrimination. (Only one bishop, as far as I know, blackballed me, not for my capacity to do a job, but because 'I don't want two high-profile woman in my area'). But far too much of my work is still listening to, and doing what I can practically to help women priests who are oppressed and atrociously treated by male priests and bishops.

People ask me, how can I remain a priest in that case? Because it is a fulfilling and joyful way of life to which the struggle for a just Church and a just society and world is integral. The Eucharist denies oppression. Celebrating the Eucharist and accepting human oppression is a contradiction which no weasle words can reconcile. A just Church could be such gloriously good news for humankind.

Before I went to St Chad's in Coventry, I was curate at St Botolph's, Aldgate. I was glad to work with Malcolm Johnson, whose team was dedicated to people at the edge, very often excluded by Church, state and populace. St Botolph's ministry was to gay and lesbian Christians, and people living homeless in London.

By the time women were first priested in 1994, I had been deacon-in-charge of St Chad's in Coventry for nine months. Bishops had appointed about a hundred deacons-in-charge of parishes by then.

I will never forget the day I first saw St Chad's. It spoke to everything that being a priest means to me. Without a vicar for almost two years, the little church looked forlorn. The vicarage was boarded up. The grass was long and littered. Broken glass sparkled in the car park; the hall had been ransacked; all its windows were broken and boarded. Fences were down. A sad-looking teenager ran away as the rural dean and I drew up. I have never felt so drawn to a place in my life; such a strong feeling of 'Oh yes! This is the place! These are the people!'

Surprisingly, no graffiti defaced the boards protecting the broken windows, only three huge words; 'Love. Joy. Peace'. The congregation wrote this, after a night of looting, when almost everything the church owned, including all its play group equipment, was carried off. In response, the church chose their own powerful graffiti.

Inside that forlorn-looking church building was a small, valiant congregation. Its members never turned away from the people around, never fell into the trap of confusing the few villainous with the many good. They belonged to, suffered with, and understood St Chad's parish, three estates then at the end of their tether – injustice in bricks and mortar, and human lives wrecked by years of poverty.

St Chad's people supported me through thick and thin. We worked together, and with anyone who would or could engage in the struggle for justice there. There, at least, the Church seems to know what its calling is; in God's name to side with the oppressed.

For the first nine months of my incumbency, friends, men, came to say the central words of the Eucharist. Their kindly action showed up the Church's tradition better than words – 'women are lesser creatures'. Thank God, and however far still to go, this was shattered at last. Coventry women were priested in April 1994.

Celebrating a Sunday Eucharist which resonates for six days of work within a community sums up being a priest for me. As a parish priest, in God's name it means being useful from birth to death. It means demanding all that makes life more abundant for the people, and denying by word and deed that oppression is God's pattern for humanity. So it means fighting alongside ill-treated tenants in the housing office, being a trusted listener, a well-informed and steely foe of the oppressor. It means connecting scripture, prayer, sacrament and action. It means finding and making friends outside the Church whose aims are the same. All these are part of the priviledge and joy of being a priest. It's a communal way of life; done with others, for God's sake. It means no denial of the Eucharist, in any sense.

Very small, ice-cold children used to come into church on Sundays. Breakfastless, thrown out, it was kindly old ladies and biscuits that brought them in. Some came for the peace and music. Many made far too much noise! I won't forget a visit from Bishop Simon Barrington-Ward. Following our custom, he gave communion into any tiny pair of grubby hands held out, and bent very low indeed, to serve them.

*   *   *

Nerissa worked as a dancer until she married David Jones, a soldier and later associate director of OXFAM, 42 years ago. They have two daughters and a son, and four grandchildren. Nerissa taught at the Ecole Francaise, Accra, Ghana, and worked in Accra psychiatric hospital during famine conditions in 1982–83, obtaining food for patients. She was educated at Bridport Grammar School, Queen Mary College, University of London and Ripon College, Cuddesdon. Ordained deacon in 1988, she served as curate at St Botolph's, Aldgate. From 1993 to 2001, she was vicar St Chad's, Wood End, Coventry, having been ordained priest in 1994. She is now incumbent of the united benefice of Askerswell, Loders and Powerstock, Dorset.

Catalyst for Change

JUDY HUNT

As the 1980s became the 1990s, I moved from vet to vicar. My veterinary work had been in a large animal surgery which was, then, a very male-dominated field of the profession, so I thought I was reasonably well-prepared to enter a second such field. That was not necessarily so! Certainly raised eyebrows and gut-reaction prejudice were encountered in both professions, but there were differences too.

'You will know them by their fruits' (Matthew 7:20, NRSV) are Gospel words which seemed to be taken more seriously in the secular farming and equestrian communities than in some sections of the Church in the early 1990s. Ability to do the job gave credibility in veterinary circles; proven expertise was valued – and such expertise was trusted more than a simple totting up of the years of experience since qualification. As a deacon and then priest during a curacy from 1991 to 1995, however, the comments from some clergy and (many fewer) lay people gave continual reinforcement of their opinion that, however fruitful the ministry of a woman priest might be, it was still suspect and second-rate.

I do believe that this attitude has been changing rapidly in more recent years: for example, I have had the joy of administering communion to clergy who would previously have absented themselves when I was presiding. They have gradually, and graciously, altered their view in the light of the fruitfulness of the ministry of ordained women. I suspect, however, that the confusion of expertise with years of experience remains fairly firmly embedded, and some posts are only open to those with a certain length of service within priests' orders. This presently affects women more than men; in future years it may affect both. If so, it will be to the detriment of the Church's work in times of challenge and change.

A second and deeply worrying difference is the legal discrimination which can still take place in the Church of England. I had not appreciated equal opportunities legislation until it was no longer relevant to me and my situation. This is not only an issue for women priests and their supporters, but I believe that it is also a suppurating sore which affects the witness of the Church in the world. Non-Church friends, contacts through occasional offices and members of adult confirmation groups have all reacted with incredulity and outrage when hearing of the Act of Synod or of the episcopate being closed to women. Their reaction has been affirming of my ministry and that of other women priests, and I have been grateful and encouraged – but also saddened by the message which goes out about the church establishment.

Being part of this church establishment, and yet also challenging it, has become a way of life – it is tiring, yet rewarding, and it requires a resilience which does not degenerate into an end state of brittleness or bitterness. This way of life has sensitized me to the plight of others in similar situations and has deepened my conviction that a Christ-centred Church is one which is truly inclusive. There is no doubt that my determination to do all that I can to bring this about has been strengthened by my own experience of being marginalized, particularly in my curacy. There is similarly no doubt that the local church family has been inspired to share these convictions, resulting in numerical growth and growth in spiritual depth. At the times when I feel profoundly discouraged, I recall services which have involved three and 83-year-olds, black and white, professors and those with great learning difficulties, those of hetero- and homo-sexual orientation, people with marked sporting talent and individuals who are physically limited . . . services where teenagers have administered communion and where those with past criminal convictions can feel welcome and contribute. I recall the way in which Jesus saw and brought out the potential in individuals, and I am given the encouragement to continue. I also recall the support I have received from Roman Catholic friends and from Roman Catholic retreat centres. The irony of feeling more at home with them than I have felt in my own denomination has injected much-needed humour into some situations!

It has been important to me to be able to meet with other women and men who share in being part of the establishment yet who believe that further change is vital. I have appreciated a number of consultations at St George's House. On one occasion someone quoted aptly from a Nelson Mandela speech:

> Our deepest fear is not that we are inadequate.
> Our deepest fear is that we are powerful beyond measure . . .
> We ask ourselves, 'Who am I to be brilliant, gorgeous, talented, fabulous?'
> Actually – who are you not to be? You are a child of God.
> Your playing small doesn't serve the world. There's nothing enlightened about shrinking so that other people won't feel insecure about you.
> We are all meant to shine . . . as we let our own light shine, we unconsciously give other people permission to do the same.

Since being priested in 1994, I, along with hundreds of other women clergy, have been this kind of a catalyst for change – whether we have wanted to be or not. The public face of the Church of England has begun to alter – the presence of women as well as men sends out messages about the Christian faith and its relevance, about its concern for justice and its openness to all. There are many (women and men) – many even within my own limited experience – who have been able to make the first steps along the journey to faith in Christ or who have been encouraged to take up the journey again simply because the Church of England has a ministry, a leadership at parish level, which is open to both genders. Just think what could happen if the Church were bold enough to go further!

* * *

Judy Hunt was born in 1957 and brought up in Lancashire. On leaving school she trained for, and then worked in, the veterinary profession, ending up as a lecturer at Liverpool Veterinary School. From 1988 to 1991 she trained for ordination and was made deacon in Chester diocese. Since then, Judy has been in parish ministry with various 'add-on' posts: Deanery Adviser for Ministry Amongst Children and Young People; Diocesan

Adviser for Women in Ministry; reader ministry responsibilities and assistant DDO. She was elected to the General Synod in 2000 and is a member of the Rural Affairs Committee.

Letter to my Father

CHRISTOPHER HALL

Father,

As you and I only ever had three adult conversations of any length, I can only guess what traumas you endured for ordaining Li Tim-Oi in 1944. Like Peter baptizing Cornelius, you only confirmed that God had already given her the gift of priesthood. After the event, you wrote to Reinhold Niebuhr saying you were 99 per cent coward, and hated disapproval from anybody. It must have hurt to be called a 'wild man of the woods' by the *Church Times* under the headline 'Bishop in Insurrection'. You were carpeted at Lambeth 1948, but my hunch is that that cost you less than hearing that Tim-Oi had resigned her priest's licence, which you had refused to withdraw at Lambeth's bidding, and that she had done so under pressure, unbidden by you, from a diocesan officer who told her it was either her or you.

You died in 1975 ten weeks before the General Synod agreed that there were no fundamental theological objections to the ordination of women. In the following debate, on whether it was then expedient to go forward, in what I expected would be my last synodical speech, I argued that it had been eminently pleasing to God that you did what you did when you did. I also told the Synod that, when I cut out from the *Church Times* its generous tribute to your life's work, I discovered that it had been printed on the other side of reports of the positive diocesan votes on the issue. Was there laughter in paradise? The next day Sir Felix Crowder thanked me for 'a "pius" speech in the classical sense of the word'.

It then took 17 years before the vote in 1992 to go forward – as long as from the crucifixion to the Council of Jerusalem's decision to admit Gentiles – 48 years since your 'cowardly' act. When the vote was announced, I was with MOW members in Central Hall Westminster, and was the quickest to do the sums on the majority in the House of Laity. Penny Nairne flung her arms around my neck.

Two years later I was invited to preach at the priesting of the first women in Banbury. I quoted from the unfinished book on priesthood you had dictated onto tape. Priesthood is always a gift from the prodigal Father, a giving of himself to the undeserving. For you priesthood was never a justice issue. One of the candidates said afterwards, 'Your father must have been a very special person.'

You may not have been happy at the efforts to include you in the Common Worship Calendar. You received more nominations than anyone else. It was decided that if you had died for Christ in the last 50 years, you were in, but not if you had but lived for him. Next time . . . ? I did get you into the Oxford Diocesan Calendar. If you are not happy about that, I hope you are that your granddaughter Frances was made deacon at Petertide.

Your 'pius' son (only in the classical sense),

Christopher

*   *   *

Born in Hong Kong, Christopher Hall has lived his life in the shadow of a saint, yet when he was 17 his father sent him this verse: 'And of two things we both I think would rather, that you were like yourself than like your father.' His father disliked church assemblies; Christopher was a member of General Synod for 19 years in all, representing the Birmingham, Manchester and Oxford dioceses, and on the Church of England Standing Committee for ten years. In those councils and in 40 years of priesthood he has championed women's ministry, ecumenism, and justice for the world's poor. The Li Tim-Oi Foundation, which he serves as secretary, has now helped more than 100 Anglican women train for Christian work in the two-thirds world.

Women at the Altar: Expressing our Common Humanity

ANN NICKSON

It began on Palm Sunday morning, my first Palm Sunday in my own parish. In line with the parish tradition, the Passion Gospel was to be read by three voices, Jesus, the evangelist, and a third voice to cover the miscellaneous characters: Peter, Judas, Pilate, Caiphas. As the parish priest, it was my task to read the words of Jesus.

As I read those words from St Matthew's Gospel, the simple yet powerful account of the institution of the Eucharist, the agonizing wrestling in Gethsemane and the climactic cry from the cross: 'Eli, Eli, Lama Sabbachtani' – all of a sudden I experienced one of those 'Aha!' moments. A moment when it's as if a light bulb comes on in your head. As a woman, reading those words of Jesus, suddenly I understood for the first time why the thought of a woman at the altar is so problematic for some; and at the same time I realized why it was so important, not just for women, but for all human beings, that a woman should stand before God at the altar. That because Christ shared our common humanity as women and men, because his cry of forsakenness sums up the cries of all the God-forsaken men, women and children throughout the world and throughout the ages, that same common humanity as women and men should be presented to God in the Eucharist.

It happened again on Maundy Thursday. In the morning I had attended the Diocesan Chrism Eucharist, sadly boycotted by male priests of the other 'integrity'. Then in the evening I had preached on the foot-washing, that prophetic act which both prefigures Christ's cross and passion and turns the expected patterns of power and authority on their heads. And then, again in line with parish tradition, it was my turn to lay aside the chasuble, take up a towel and kneel to wash the feet of the 12 'disciples' gathered before me. A mixed bunch of people, no doubt much like the original 12, except now there were women and men, black and white, old and young, gnarled elderly feet and smooth manicured feet. After the foot-washing, again in line with parish tradition, the 12 joined me in the sanctuary for the eucharistic prayer, and the words of institution that we had just heard read in the Maundy Thursday epistle struck me with new force and power.

I was ordained priest in 1999, five years after the first priestings; the priestings of the women who had waited and hoped and at times come close to despair. For my generation of women priests things have been different, although I suspect most of us carry the burden of feeling the need not to fail; the need to be better than male colleagues if we are to receive the same opportunities. A male priest, whatever his tradition, doctrinal stance or quality of life, is always acceptable. As women, regardless of our qualifications, gifts or abilities, for some we will never be acceptable. And so the temptation is to struggle to be better, to work longer hours, never to turn down an opportunity to speak or join a diocesan working party. I long for the day when a woman priest can be indifferent or even poor and no one think any more about it than we do when we encounter a mediocre male priest.

And yet, three years on from my own priesting my overriding sense is of gratitude. Gratitude to God for the opportunity to fulfil my vocation as a priest. Gratitude to groups like MOW and to all the women who, inspired by the Spirit, struggled and persevered. Gratitude also to the male priests who stood with us. Those like the founder members of the Society of Catholic Priests, who in 1994 left SSC to form a new society which would welcome and affirm the ministry of women; a place of fellowship and mutual respect where gender increasingly seems irrelevant. I'm grateful, too, to my training incumbent, to the parishioners I have sought to serve and to the non-church-goers whose weddings or funerals I have taken. So often I've heard the comment, 'We were surprised to find that you were a woman' and I've felt myself tense, waiting for the other shoe to drop, only to find warmth, affirmation and acceptance.

*   *   *

Ann Nickson was born in Bolton in 1958. After studying law in Cambridge, she trained as a solicitor, becoming a litigation partner in a practice in Bromley. The untimely death of a close friend in 1987 led to a re-examination of priorities and eventually the decision to respond to a persistent sense of vocation. She trained for ordination at Ridley Hall and after obtaining a first in theology, worked for a PhD on the theology of Dietrich Bonhoeffer (published as *Bonhoeffer on Freedom*, Ashgate, 2002). Ann was ordained in 1998 and after a curacy in the Sanderstead team ministry, became priest-in-charge of St Stephen Norbury and Thornton Heath in 2001. She teaches doctrine at the South East Institute for Theological Education. Ann shares her vicarage with a somewhat disturbed but affectionate cat.

At the Interface Between the World and the Kingdom

HELEN CUNLIFFE

I'm writing this at St Mary's Convent, Wantage. There is an appropriateness about this, for it's here I came, aged 17, as I tried to make sense of God's call, if indeed it was God's call, and not some romantic notion best laid to rest. Faith has been important to me for as long as I can remember, and I have delighted in those moments of connection with other people on the same Way. It has always been a joy to be in God's house, though not always in God's Church.

There was, as for any woman of my age and older, a problem in discerning and then responding to God's call. The religious life in its totality never looked likely, though it remains a vital resource – what then? At first I was not aware of wanting to be a priest; all I wanted was a place in which to grow closer to God, and bring others there too. I'm still not sure I want to be a priest, if that means serving the Church as it is, in ways that seem alien to me. But if priesthood means, as of course it does for many, placing oneself deliberately and consistently at interfaces between this world's values and those of the kingdom, and helping to resource those who stand there daily, then that is what I want to do. Priesthood for me is to do with handing over the keys to the kingdom – giving every grown-up Christian his or her set of front door keys, welcoming them into the house, expecting them to want to rearrange the furniture and put up their own pictures: 'in my Father's house are many rooms'.

Opening the kingdom and setting God free from too many words and constructions, seems a useful work to be about. The hardest times – the hardest places to be, and the hardest people to be with – have been when this desire to serve God, couched in such terms, has been mistaken as irreverent, insufficiently learned or informed, as somehow not serious enough – not 'proper'. It has been hard to be dismissed, corrected, not made very welcome, because I was unwilling to conform to the shape the Church mostly seems to want me to be. There have been some dark times, and I don't see them getting much lighter in the immediate future. It never fails to shock and disturb me how subversive women priests are experienced as being. So many checks on us seem to be needed, so many safeguards against us. The Act of Synod remains, creating an atmosphere of 'here on approval' for all ordained women, however happy their present, particular situation. Women bishops would be the simplest thing in the world to achieve, if the will were there; here are women, and here is the calling of 'bishop'. One is reminded of the eunuch's challenge to Philip. Instead, theology must be carefully gone over, all over again – as if to count up how many reasons one can find for not simply getting on with it. Even in the most enlightened settings there still seems to be a problem – one female church warden is very good, two is 'petticoat government'. One woman on a cathedral chapter is plenty – I can't think of any places where there are two. I don't know why we put up with it. We must either be mad, or else really rather faithful.

Of course I do know why we put up with it. Those we've ministered to over the years, and presently do, make it more than worthwhile. In 18 years of ministry I have loved those moments when God has been recognized as present among us. Countless ordinary human moments, high and low, private and public, have been precious as times when we have been aware of God's love and God's closeness. I have much to be grateful for, and glad about. I look forward to the time when living in God's house and being in the Church can feel like the same place, and can feel like home.

*   *   *

Born in Derbyshire in 1954, Helen was educated at Homelands School, Derby, and at St Hilda's College, Oxford. She married Christopher in 1979. She trained for ministry at Westcott House, Cambridge, from 1981 to 1983, and was made a deaconess in 1983. She job-shared a curacy at Chesterfield parish church, and shared bringing up Edward, born in 1983, with Christopher. She was deaconess on the staff of the University Church, Oxford, from 1986 to 1989, during which time Jacob was born in 1988. Also during this time she was chaplain of Nuffield College. She then became deacon-in-charge of St Paul's, Clapham, and was vicar from 1994 to 1996 (although the licence had to say 'team member'). She has been residentiary Canon of Southwark Cathedral – styled Canon Pastor – since 1996 and is Diocesan Advisor for Women in Ministry. Since writing this piece, Helen has been appointed Archdeacon of St Albans.

Reflecting Priesthood

CARRIE PEMBERTON

'How marvellous!', 'Well done', 'You're different', 'Lovely to meet a happy one' have been some of the posies and accolades along the path of the priesthood which now spans just under a decade. The comment that 'This is my first time' had about it the quality of surprise and vulnerability of my greying male host's first romance. And most of this, the substantial lion's share of this paean of praise has absolutely nothing to do with who I am, what I as a person, with my history, my story, my thoughts and emotions, prayers and dreams, bring to the priesthood. No – it is simply the fact that I am a woman, and while a woman, a priest. This juxtaposition has nuclear fission power. It both attracts substantial comment and interest, yet still has the power to evoke fear.

Disappearing behind the collar, becoming simultaneously highly visible and yet personally invisible, has been a strap-line of my life. Growing up in a clergy home, my father bluff and politically astute, cut a splendid figure in black clericals and startling white collar underscoring his dazzling teeth. My mother, National Homes of Britain housewife, church floral decorator extraordinaire and tin box collection amasser, would stand at some distance with her clutch of children, regaling all and sundry with our many gifts and attributes, while I disappeared into the inner conversation of childhood. Our 1950s church which my father had seen designed and built as part of the reconstruction of the London suburbs in the decades after the war, held little for me by way of interest or comfort in its liturgical life. There were always bills to be paid, fund-raising initiatives to put in place, petty fights within Parochial Church Councils to resolve, disgruntled parishioners to placate.

The airy space of St Mary's Church, Shortlands, with its high vaulted ceilings and peeling white paint, held a quiet fascination for me, while my mother watered the pedestal vases and worried over the fading lilies. Maybe climbing the steps to the light oak pulpit one day found me at eight years old, day-dreaming about being a vicar like my father – I was a tomboy after all and never troubled myself with aspirations in floral displays or housewifery. As I peered over the deep ledge designed to carry the package of books without which no Church of England service seems to be able to commence, my two cats, brought into the cool sanctity of the church in a makeshift cardboard cat-carrier, looked back at me quizzically. They had obviously never heard of women in ministry either. I knew we had an ancient woman missionary working in Uganda, because she sent letters to the church every so often which my father would refer to in his sermons when he wasn't extolling the virtues of some ancient city called Dunkirk. This town which I believed must be somewhere between London and Dover, was of central importance to Christianity, the essence of what it meant to be British and the medicament of choice for our churches. I could never quite follow its relevance. I filed it away alongside the prophetic and somewhat political words of the 1662 prayer book where God had declared himself to be the 'lover of Concorde'.

Several hundred real-time sermons and numerous offerings of the Eucharist later, what is the meaning of women in priestly clothing, which might cause my mother dutifully watering her flowers, or my late father with his guns and glory texts, to take note? Little has changed and yet much has shifted. As my three daughters find themselves exploring churches and meeting congregations, they know that if they wanted to they could become vicars, chaplains, ministers like their mother. They don't spend time reflecting and playing in the house of God while Mum waters the lilies of the field which would otherwise wither. I work a long 50–55 hour week, visiting, counselling, pursuing advocacy, bringing some dreams nearer reality, helping people to pray, preaching and attending meetings. I am more absent than my mother, more fulfilled at one turn, more distracted at another. My daughters' world has few moments of creative boredom and is yet full of potential. They were birthed in the age of equal opportunity. Like myself as a child, they can don a tea cosy and understand themselves to be bishops, popes and cardinals.

Like my adult self, they should be given the chance to contribute their insight, their womanly wisdom, their compassion and energies into leadership and service to whichever threshold their abilities take them. But these organizational and cultural circumstances are not yet in place in Mother Church.

The Dunkirk spirit which informed so much of my father's spirituality, seems to lurk within the mentality of the English Church and its reading of organizational polity. It was, after all, men who took up the political and military leadership which drove this country into war with the great European superpower in 1939. Although the Iron Lady was clearly at the helm in 1976 with the Falklands conflict, it is still substantially men who prepare, brief, plan and execute warfare across the continents. Similarly in the world of 'Onward Christian Soldiers', we march as to war, with a fleet of male colonels in chief at the helm, scarcely pausing to consider whether warfare is necessarily the metaphor we wish to see as our controlling motif. Moreover these World War I style generals seem heedless or at best impotent to stem the tide of rank-and-file soldiery vacating the trenches.

Co-operation and reconciliation seem more in accordance with the earthly Jesus, and just as much a miracle as when Jesus promised the presence of the kingdom of heaven to two or three of his assembled preening disciples. For women who have been in so many ways subalterned along with the rank-and-file of men to a practice of church which is about power, status, and feeling good or safe about ourselves, even when so much of our older formal liturgy reminds us how totally unworthy we are, we have an immense challenge which endures.

The freedom of spirit which slumbers in all of us, waits to be awakened afresh with a clarion of imagination which fervently challenges the nonsense of patriarchy and the closure of episcopacy to contemporary women. If we are to be a Church which speaks to my daughters as well as my sons, we must respond to their experience of diversity of gifts, and equality of opportunity. The Dunkirk spirit has gone the way of the Chelsea Pensioners, and in a few years all that will be left will be the strains of a melody with no one marching in time to its beat. We are in desperate need of a new vision of what Christian faith can deliver in an age of nano-second technological change, fragmented communities, and the moneterization of pleasure, ethics and cultures.

Jesus began by calling 12 disciples and their households as his interns. A new community calls us. A community which traverses the shores of these islands, includes the laughter of children in playgrounds around the world, the tears of others behind the doors of dysfunctional homes, the memory of women with sturdy footwear, the steady breath of God who inspired the early Church to recognize neither male nor female, Jew nor Greek, slave nor free, but that all are one in Christ Jesus. The shape of such a community is unclear, the call from its centre is irrevocable. That is the nuclear fission power of the future. The only way to tap into its energy is to put the atom of our inequalities back together again.

* * *

Carrie Pemberton was ordained deacon in 1987 and worked with the Anglican Church in D.R. Congo (formerly Zaire) as Director of Women's Development and lecturer in systematics at the Institut Superieur Theologique Anglican. While completing her doctorate in African Women's Theologies at the University of Cambridge, Carrie worked non-stipendiarily as a priest alongside her husband before taking up a position at the University of Cambridge exploring contemporary currents in World Christianity. She was subsequently appointed the first ecumenical minister of Cambourne – an IT hub development – her first salaried appointment since ordination as a deacon a decade before. She currently works full-time in immigration control as a religious manager and chaplain. An author on gender issues in theology, worldwide Anglicanism and structural violence in church and home, Carrie trains in cross-cultural awareness, spirituality in business and in the issues surrounding family–life balance. She is married to a fellow priest and has five children and a big personality dog in a small frame. She is the e-chaplain for www. Everywoman.co.uk.

Moving Further to the Margins

SUSAN SHIPP

We were a momentary focus in early 1994. The media buzzed around us, fascinated by this shift of gender emphasis within the national Church. On that magnificent ordination day in March, what few seemed to recognize, and no one recorded, was that, as T.S. Eliot writes in 'Four Quartets', we were 'still and still moving'. Momentarily, and historically, we were caught on film, in the midst of sacrament and worship, but essentially we were on pilgrimage – the ordination service a profound marking along a way we still travel. The newspaper clippings, articles of broadsheet and tabloid, and the video films in French and German remain tucked away in a drawer, waiting to be sorted, and stored as befits such famous archive material. That is how it should be, for I have moved on.

Following ordination I felt like a pot-holer discovering a further, deeper subterranean passage, which had been there all the time, waiting to be found and travelled. Yet after nearly 20 years of ministry, first as a religious, and now as a priest, the track I'm taking leads me along the edge, away from the centre of church life to the marketplace of chaplaincy. Here, who I am, and who I may become, is more important than what I am; nothing can be taken for granted.

The journey so far has been hard, but that was to be expected: 'What did you go out into the wilderness to see?' Since ordination, the deeper awareness that priesthood is not gender specific, has been confirmed, so that my role models are both male and female, and those particularly who work on the edge, going unrecognized, blowing open the narrower understandings of what priesthood is about.

In 1999, looking for a new appointment, I was offered a choice of remaining a parish priest, or of becoming a hospital chaplain. Taking the route of chaplain has led me along rugged tracks, with glorious, if occasionally perilous, views. For me, as for the bishop who first said it to me, priesthood is a way of life, a way of being, a way of looking out upon and living within the world, an expanding vocation of discovery and service. I sense that, if I have sufficient courage, the track I'm now taking will lead me further into less charted territory.

Amid the wonders and perils of the journey so far, a sadness continues to dog my steps. The sadness is in relation to the institution which continues to be gender-bound, allowing unfounded prejudice and fear to hold sway, so preserving the outdated images of the Church of England. In 1994 we had high hopes that, not far beyond ten years, a female bishop would be consecrated. Currently, that hope will have to be sustained for far longer. For myself, as for many women priests, the journey will not be complete until such a consecration takes place.

*   *   *

Susan Shipp spent three formative years testing her vocation to the religious life in South Africa. Returning to Britain in 1979, she commenced training for the ordained ministry at Lincoln Theological College in 1981. Having attended university in Wales, though not Welsh, Susan returned to Wales in 1983 where she was ordained to the diaconate, serving her title in a team ministry on the outskirts of Cardiff before returning to England, and the diocese of Bristol in 1987. Since 1989 Susan has served in a wide variety of parishes, while also undertaking diocesan work as ecumenical officer, and serving on Bishop's Council. Susan served national ecumenical interests by being a member of the Local Unity Committee, and latterly as a member of the Anglican–Moravian Committee. Before leaving parochial ministry for hospital chaplaincy in 1999, Susan was incumbent of Longwell Green, diocesan ecumenical officer, and honorary canon of Bristol Cathedral. Susan is now senior co-ordinating chaplain within the West Hertfordshire Hospitals NHS Trust.

Discovering New Patterns

FAITH CLARINGBULL

God is calling the Church to new patterns of ministry, not just in order for the institution to survive, but so that the whole of who we are as God's people may be embraced, used and celebrated. The circumstances of my life these past ten years have led me to weave new patterns with the threads of who I believe God has called me to be – a priest, a wife and a mother.

A photograph appeared on the front page of the *Guardian* the day after the vote – Nerissa Jones and myself on the steps of Church House, Westminster, embracing one another with overwhelming joy. My husband, Keith, is in the picture too. The issue of women's ordination to the priesthood has never been just for me and my fulfilment. It is not just for women and our equality. It is an issue for both women and men in the Church. I continue to hope that the inclusion of women in the priesthood will release both women and men to be more the people God intends us to be. I am grateful to Wendy Robinson who has helped many of us explore some of these tricky, but creative, gender issues. Now the frame contains the priestly ministry of both myself and Keith. In Sue Walrond-Skinner's words, 'managing the two covenants of marriage and ministry requires new thinking for a new situation', not just for us personally, but for the whole Church (*Double Blessing*, Mowbray, 1998, p. 229).

Another photograph was taken on the steps of St Paul's Cathedral after my ordination. Our four-month-old daughter is in my arms. Alan Webster is in the background handing out champagne in plastic cups. What committed and loving mid-wives Alan and Margaret were to women's ordination! Because I was breast-feeding Rachel, she needed to come with me on the ordination retreat. I was delighted to receive from the Bishop of London, David Hope, a cheque out of his discretionary fund for the childcare I had organized which enabled me to attend the worship and addresses.

Since I was ordained deacon in 1989 my sense of calling to be a priest has remained unchanged. However, my ministry has expressed itself in different ways because of family circumstances: stipendiary and non-stipendiary, parish, hospital chaplaincy and diocesan, full-time, job-share and part-time. It is important that in the debate on the future of ministry we are careful to distinguish between a call to priesthood and modes of deployment. The Church needs to be creative and flexible. These are exciting times, if we dare to embrace the challenge.

I have disappointments. I am disappointed when women have not found new ways of doing church. It is a hard, costly and often lonely journey. The ministry of friendship and encouragement is precious. It is one that has enabled me to be who I am, and I value it to sustain me where I am. It is a ministry that is not exclusive to women, but it is one in which we are gifted. We must cherish and exercise this ministry within the Church. Women need to encourage one another to apply for senior posts and support one another in difficult ministries. Many challenges remain: to break down barriers of hierarchy, to challenge ways of functioning by committee, to make more accessible the way the Church works. Much has changed, but I remain impatient. I am grateful to Penny Jamieson and her book *Living at the Edge*, 'which is essentially about the dynamics that occur when the edges of a particularly strong patriarchal institution are pushed and the vision of what God's Church could be are expanded' (Mowbray, 1997, p. 6).

I am worried that so many of the new generation of women seem not to see or even experience the challenges and injustices that remain within the Church. The experience of returning to theological college was a curious one. Ten years on, most female ordinands appear to have had, and appear to expect, plain sailing. However, the Church of England remains an institution exempt from the Sex Discrimination Act of 1975 and subsequent equal rights legislation. Many women of my generation who are wearied by the struggle for the ordination of women would be glad if some younger women would now help to carry the baton for change.

Despite these disappointments, I remain hopeful. A number

of experiences in recent years remind me that time and place can be redeemed, that we must celebrate the good news and that indeed the kingdom is coming. The college principal, John Clarke, invited me to preside at the Eucharist in the chapel at Cuddesdon. It was a place where in the late 1980s I had sat in various degrees of pain, knowing my calling to be a priest but having that neither recognized by the Church nor respected by a number of fellow ordinands. To stand behind the altar in that place was an immensely powerful and healing experience and to (re)claim the ground, not just for myself, was an unexpected privilege.

My father died just two months before my ordination. He had remained opposed to the ordination of women as priests. I have inherited a set of his stoles and I wore one when I laid hands on Keith at his ordination in Worcester Cathedral in 2001. I had a powerful sense of taking my place in the line of priests who have stood there over the centuries performing just such an action. It felt the right place for a woman to be.

Christina Baxter led a meditation on the raising of Lazarus during our ordination retreat. A conversation with her helped to move a stone and enabled me to walk freely to my ordination. I am enormously grateful to those women and men who, along my journey and along the journey of the ordination of women, have moved stones in order that new life might emerge, who have helped to unbind us and set us free and who have called us out of the shadows into new ways of being and new patterns of ministry.

           *   *   *

Having worked as a librarian, Faith trained for ordination at Ripon College Cuddesdon. She was ordained in 1989 and became parish deacon on the Isle of Dogs where she married Keith. While a chaplain at the Royal London Hospital she was ordained priest and had two children, Rachel and Anna. In 1998 Faith returned to Cuddesdon where Keith trained and she was an NSM in a nearby parish. Since 2000, she has been quarter-time Assistant Diocesan Director of Ordinands in Worcester. She also works as a voluntary chaplain at St Richard's Hospice and assists in the parish of Inkberrow as a member of the local ministry team.

Ongoing Transformation

CAROLINE DICK

My daughter, Katrina, was just four weeks old on 11 November 1992 when the vote to ordain women as priests was passed. She was asleep at the time, but I picked her up out of the Moses basket by way of letting her 'know' that something momentous had happened. When Katrina was baptized into the Church three months later, I felt an overwhelming sense of joy, because I knew that the body of which she had become a part was one that now recognized her full stature as a daughter of God. I knew that I wasn't going to have to spend a lifetime explaining why Mummy couldn't do certain things that Daddy (who is a priest) could, but above all, I knew that the old order which I had found so stifling and oppressive as a woman was now passing away and a new order beginning.

I wrote those words for a booklet that was produced to mark the occasion of the first 38 women being made priests in the diocese of Durham in May 1994. At that time I had just begun work as assistant chaplain at the University of Sunderland, and I couldn't have got off to a better start!

Normally the role of chaplain is a fairly low-key one, and it takes a while to be known and accepted, but I literally had students crossing the street to speak to me, because they wanted to know if I was one of those new things called a 'woman priest'. It was a bit like being a mini-celebrity. I was asked to take part in a radio interview, and complete strangers would stop me or ring up to say, 'Well done, it's wonderful.'

I think people really sensed that for once the Church was doing something liberating, fresh, new and relevant. It was seen to be on the side of life, and prepared to engage with contemporary reality. It was letting some fresh air in, and blowing some old cobwebs away.

Looking back they were heady days.

Many of the men who were in favour of women priests felt that their own priesthood was now complete and renewed, and they wanted to join with us in creating something genuinely transformative. This verse from the Iona community's hymn: 'Shake up the morning' captures some of the hopes and dreams that were around at the time:

Shake up the Church and let all Christians show,
That faith is real, that God is good to know;
Fashion new symbols of the coming age
When hope and love will take the centre stage.
Praise to the Lord whose Gospel we inherit;
Praise God's bird of love, the Holy Spirit;
Praise to the Son whose will and words decree
All are one in his community.

A new symbol was forged when women were made priests, a symbol of equality, of inclusivity, of mutuality and of the fullness of humanity revealed in the Godhead, and that symbol continues to grow and develop. Inevitably, ten years down the line, women priests are (broadly speaking) an accepted part of the ecclesiastical landscape, and our presence has been normalized. Women have radically changed the way in which priesthood is perceived and exercised, but the larger task of transforming the male, hierarchical institution of which we are a part is proving as difficult as ever.

I currently work as the diocese of Durham's Board of Social Responsibility's Development Officer, and it was partly in that capacity that I was elected onto General Synod in September 2000. As I said at the time 'serving the central structures of the Church of England has never been at the top of my agenda, but keeping the world on the Church's agenda certainly is!' I was also finally persuaded to stand because I knew that if I didn't, there would be no woman standing in the House of Clergy from our diocese, and I believe that we have to make the most of the opportunities that we have been given to speak prophetically into the Church structures.

Now perhaps more than at any other time in recent church history, we are tempted to focus all our energies on a survival strategy for the Church as an institution, whereas I believe that we should be directing the Church's energies into a survival strategy for the world, which is perpetually on the brink of self-destruction and environmental catastrophe. Jubilee 2000 gave the Church a wonderful model of good practice in this respect. Through it we were seen to be visible, prophetic, relevant, ecumenical and powerful in the best sense, i.e. we weren't approaching it as a holy crusade, but as part of a global coalition that cares passionately about God's creation.

I thank God for my calling to the priesthood and the way in which I am being shaped by it and by others. If I had to sum up where my journey into priesthood has taken me, it would be in the form of this blessing written by an unknown author from Canada:

> May God bless you with discomfort at easy answers, half-truths, superficial relationships, so that you will live deep within your heart.
> May God bless you with anger at injustice, oppression and exploitation of people, so that you will work for justice, equity and peace.
> May God bless you with tears to shed for those who suffer from pain, rejection, starvation and war, so that you will reach out your hand to comfort them and change their pain to joy.
> May God bless you with the foolishness to think that you can make a difference in the world, so that you will do the things which others tell you cannot be done.

*   *   *

Caroline Dick is 41 years old and married to Raymond, the vicar of St Peter's Church in Harton, South Shields. They have two children, Katrina, who is ten, and Jonathan, who is seven. Caroline was ordained deacon in 1988 and has served in the diocese of Durham ever since. After a curacy at Houghton-le-Spring, she became assistant chaplain at the University of Sunderland, and is now working for the Board of Social Responsibility. She spent a year as vice-chair of National WATCH and is currently a member of General Synod, and the Advisor in Women's Ministry in Durham diocese.

Challenge and Liberation

RACHEL WOOD

It had never crossed my mind to become an ordained minister in the Church of England until I watched the debate and vote about women priests on the television in November 1992. I was volunteering for the mission charity USPG near Walsall at the time and had been a fervent Christian at my university Christian Union, but I'd not previously felt a call to priesthood. The vote for women priests changed this, because now it was a reality. The vote meant there were going to be women priests and, as a woman, I could be one of them. Despite my lack of awareness of the long struggle to get the motion passed, I cried when the decision was 'Yes'. It felt like a 'Yes' to me and a 'Yes' to women generally, a real sign that God loved women too and wanted them to take an active role in the leadership of the Church and to help bring new insights and perspectives to the Church and to society.

It was another four years before I started my training and another four before I was ordained priest. The person that watched the vote then feels a long way away from the person I am now. But the vote showed me something of the issues that are still important to me; the challenge and freedom the gospel brings and the tensions and opportunities that exist for me as a priest in the Church of England.

The Church of England has been run almost exclusively by men for the whole of its existence. I believe this makes the Church of England an androcentric institution, part of an androcentric tradition and culture. The problems that arise from this affect both men and women, who become bound up in a prescriptive culture with definite and restricting role models. As a woman priest I am part of and shaped by the Church. I have colluded with the institution but can also, I hope, challenge it.

It is in my own relationship with the power structures and

those who hold power in the Church where I find my struggle to liberate and challenge come to the fore. In ministry I found the curate/incumbent relationship a very difficult one to navigate. In my first curacy I found myself unable to challenge what I perceived as my incumbent's controlling behaviour. In wider clergy meetings I felt my suggestions were unheard, my calls for change dismissed. This seems to be a symptom of a patriarchal institution and has been the experience of many friends and colleagues, both men and women. When I felt it was no longer helpful for me to stay in my first post and asked to move, the primary response was not 'How can we help?', but 'How dare you challenge the system!' However, it also became clear to me in this situation that I had to take my own responsibility for the perceived problems and find new ways to challenge. I had to develop my own strategies, instead of swallowing my anger and frustration to the point of depression when my often too timid questions were ignored.

However, the fact that I am not the 'norm', that I am a young(ish) woman priest, can sometimes have the effect of releasing others to see things in a new way too. In leading worship and preaching, just the fact of a woman's voice which seeks to offer a perspective rooted in the faith but also our culture and experience has, I've been told, broadened people's understanding of themselves and God, helped people see their faith in new ways. In pastoral situations too, I have experienced surprising emotional responses. After leading a funeral I was overwhelmed at the door when the previously very buttoned-up South Yorkshire widower threw himself into my arms sobbing heavily.

The tenth anniversary of the vote to ordain women as priests is a cause of great celebration. In my brief experience change has been slow but real. It continues to require energy to hold onto my own vision of my role as one who might challenge and enable liberation in the Church, but the opportunities and possibilities in ministry are, I believe, as many as I allow them to be.

*   *   *

Rachel Wood was born in 1971. She was brought up in the North East before going to the University of Birmingham to study English. She then became a member of a USPG Root

Group near Walsall in 1992–93 when the vote was passed. After this initial call to ordained ministry she worked in community and homeless projects in Manchester and Rochdale. Upon being accepted for ordination she began training for ministry at Queen's College, Birmingham in 1996. Her first curacy was in an inner-city parish in east Sheffield and she is currently in her second curacy in a suburban area of Leeds.

Good for Women – Good for the Church and the World

DAVID DRISCOLL

Many of the stories surrounding the events that took place on that amazing day ten years ago will no doubt appear in this book. On the actual day, 11 November 1992, I was on a list of people to be interviewed by the BBC on Radio 4, and was actually called into one of the radio studios at Church House just as the vote was being taken! I was shaking all over, but tried my hardest to sound as calm as possible. I remember suggesting that in a short space of time people would be wondering what all the fuss was about.

The following day I had to attend a routine pastoral committee meeting, and somehow everything felt different. The future for the Church of England now seemed so bright. So am I happy at the way things have turned out? Certainly in my former parish people took women priests totally in their stride when an ordained woman colleague joined our woman lay reader and myself, and this heralded six years of very rewarding and enriching ministry. Very early on, warm expressions of appreciation of her ministry got back to me, often from the most unlikely of quarters. This reinforced for me, if it needed reinforcing, the conviction how incomplete, as men priests, our ministry had been before the vote. Other parishes in the deanery were also appointing women priests, and this dramatically transformed our deanery clergy chapter for the better.

We were fortunate too not to have any parishes in our deanery opting out. There were definitely no alternative chapters! I was aware, however, of the pain and division in other deaneries caused by the Act of Synod. When my deanery synod was presented with the simple facts of the Act, synod members were quite appalled and in a subsequent debate voted overwhelmingly for it to be rescinded as soon as possible. I expect other contributors will comment on the unfortunate effects of the Act and suggest what steps should be taken for its rescinding. I am also very much aware of the desirability of women bishops in the Church of England and continue to be associated with the campaign.

Apart from their theological rightness, the achievement of these two goals would do much to remove the institutional sexism still prevalent in our Church. Both goals could also be perceived as merely clerical and parochial concerns, considering the vast majority of the Church, 99.9 per cent of them, are laity, of whom more than 50 per cent are women. Are there other goals which we ought to be striving for? If we merely focus on women clergy are we not at the same time neglecting other glaringly obvious ways in which women are still being exploited?

One thing I had hoped for after the vote was a less introspective Church of England, but although there have been honourable exceptions, nothing much seems to have changed. For example, I would love to see our Church working alongside people and groups trying to tackle the enormous international problem of the mistreatment and abuse of women in the South, where so many women live in abject poverty and are denied basic human rights. In many of these places women do most of the work and receive very little of the reward, and becoming a widow, apart from the sense of personal loss, leads to a life of degradation and misery. Most of us cannot possibly begin to imagine the suffering they endure.

There are NGOs and groups working extremely hard to change the lot of women throughout the world, and this is surely a 'kingdom' issue. It is interesting how many people engaged in such work were once Christian, but sadly have given up on their faith because Christianity, as currently practised, seems to have no relevance to the vital work they are doing. In all honesty, how far up the list of the Church's present priorities is the alleviation of the hardship millions of women all over the world have to endure?

So what do I hope and pray for over the next ten years? First, I am convinced we need women bishops, and second, we really must do something about the Act of Synod for the future health of the Church of England. Lastly, I still retain a vision of Christians being alongside their sisters and brothers of good will, whatever their faith or lack of it, and also with fellow Anglicans and other Christians all over the world, trying to tackle the terrible injustices still being done to women. It is an enormous task, but if we make an attempt, then the Church will rightly be seen as an authentic sign of the kingdom of God.

* * *

Canon David Driscoll served for 30 years in the diocese of Chelmsford, first as a chaplain in higher education, then in an inner-city parish, finally becoming vicar of St Mary's, Theydon Bois. He was engaged in adult lay education in the diocese and representing the diocese in the World Church activities specializing in the Caribbean. Before ordination he taught in Pakistan with VSO, returning to the UK to become a regional secretary with the Student Christian Movement. He has been actively committed to women's ministry and served on the national executive of WATCH and is currently honorary development officer of the Modern Churchpeople's Union. He has recently moved diocese to become associate vicar of All Hallows by the Tower in the City of London.

Affirmation and Acceptance

DAVID HAWTIN

On the morning after the 11 November vote, I emerged tired and bleary-eyed from the London hotel where I was staying, ready to head off for another day's business as a General Synod representative. The sun was shining – certainly in my heart and, I think, from the sky. This particular morning I noticed the women going to work – to London's shops, offices and institutions. Many of them were young, with their eyes set on the future. I said to myself, 'Yes, I can face you, because the Church of England has made a decision to move forward and to be part of that future. Women, alongside men, will be part of our Church's priestly leadership.'

As a member of the Movement for the Ordination of Women and of its Synod Steering Group, I had been deeply involved not only in hope and vision, but also in the detail of synodical strategy and tactics. Having had an eye on detail for such a long time, I emerged that morning to rediscover the significance of the decision now made – that as a Church we could retain credibility and integrity in witnessing to a gospel that speaks to the whole of humanity and to the emerging future. It may be hard to argue that the Church of England is, or is seen to be, in the forefront of radical social witness in its public ministry, but at least in deciding to ordain women to the priesthood we were keeping in touch with developments in society. The decision was one for mission.

Having been appointed archdeacon at the beginning of 1992, I had kept my diary clear for the Sunday after the vote so that I could decide which church to attend that day. I went to worship with a congregation where the clergy and most of the congregation were opposed to the decision made three days earlier. There I experienced the numbed shock of those who felt the tremor of the Church changing beneath them. The decision was divisive. Since those early days, General Synod has strengthened the provision already existing in the legislation by introducing a pattern of extended episcopal ministry for parishes through the Act of Synod. While the November 1992 vote affirmed the priestly vocation of women, the way in which the Act of Synod has been used by some has undermined that affirmation.

But affirmation there certainly has been. I think of three women colleagues in the diocese where I served as archdeacon, and of their ministry before and after the vote. Before, each was serving as deacon. One had offered ministry in a tough and hurting urban community where no man was rushing to serve. Another was a much-loved pastor in the countryside with a group of churches. The third was a hospital chaplain, required in a secular environment to show professional expertise, discipline and accountability to a degree well beyond that of the usual parish priest. Their competence was never in doubt. Their ordination to the priesthood in 1994 (maybe you remember that slow 'grind to joy' between 1992 and 1994) was the sacramental and public endorsement of the full ministry which they wished to offer the Church. Acknowledged by those among whom they worked, they were no longer restricted by the Church.

In the years since the vote, I have in my role as archdeacon and in my ministry as bishop seen the priestly ministry of women take root in the Church of England – in some cases, not without pain and significant loss, but often with great fulfilment and satisfaction – along with the boredom, routine and frustration which also feature in ordained ministry!

The positives have been in mission, affirmation and acceptance. To say that the Church of England has held together is also a positive, but there needs to be some recognition of the cost involved, and of the spirituality needed to sustain the arrangements permitted by the Act of Synod. Comprehensiveness in the Church of England is a costly and loving vocation to shared living, not a device for legitimized separateness.

There are two particular areas where we need progress, and neither is likely to be achieved through legislation. First, the culture of the Church of England remains largely male. We do things in much the same way as we did before the decision to include women in the priestly leadership of the Church. That may be less the case where women have a clear leadership role, most obviously in parish life, when the dynamic of personal relationships can become significantly different, and when the style of worship may change. But the Church of England – like many other institutions in society – retains its traditional male way of operating. We need to learn that there are other ways of doing business, and to be patient about the change and exploration required.

Second, ordained women remain a visual and audible minority in the way that the Church gathers its representatives together. We all recognize that women are the majority in our congregations, but this becomes less so as we go further into our representative synods and decision-making bodies. Among the ordained, women are a numerical minority, but in addition they are dispersed widely across our church groups – one, two or three, or none at all, among rural deans, cathedral clergy canons, and bishop's staff members.

For both these reasons, we need to keep in place and develop appointments which highlight women's ministry as a key contribution to the life and behaviour of the Church. It is no good concluding that 'the job's done' just because women are now ordained priest. Priesthood is pervasive. In other words, it is not a closed esoteric constituency, but a sign of the fullness of our humanity in Christ. An important step has been taken with the ordination of women to the priesthood, but much remains to be done to make the consequences of that decision impact on the Church at all points.

* * *

David Hawtin has been Bishop of Repton in the diocese of Derby since 1999. He served for 25 years in Durham diocese in four parishes and as a full-time ecumenical officer between 1988 and 1992. He was appointed archdeacon of Newark in 1992.

He served as a member of General Synod in 1983–99. He is deeply involved in the movement for Christian unity, especially through Churches Together in England, and in the areas of ministerial training and development, and of community and social engagement. The spirituality of Taizé is a continuing source of inspiration.

New Awakenings

CHRISTOPHER COCKSWORTH

It could have been a difficult situation. I was a newly ordained deacon. Mavis was a deacon as well. She was also married to the vicar, Mark Wilson. The relational dynamics were hazardous. How would I fit into this husband and wife team? How would I fit into the parish? How would Mavis begin to develop a distinctively ordained ministry in this parish where she was a well-established vicar's wife? How would she receive me? How would Mark receive me? What space would there be for the three of us in this parish at this time in the Church of England's history? Would there come a day when Mavis would be ordained priest? My time, I knew, would come, and come soon – how would we handle the joy and pain of all that?

We knew that history was slowly unfolding before our eyes. And we knew that in the strange ways in which God's will is woven through the actions of ordinary human beings in ordinary places, how we handled those relationships would become part of the raw material of ordinary opinion that would help make up the Church's mind. But much of this was left unsaid, largely, so it seemed to me, because Mavis, by herself and with Mark, embodied an extraordinary gifting to trust in the power of loving. John Chrysostom in the fourth century ran away from being ordained because he knew that he did not yet know the 'power of love' as the life-blood of Christian ministry. Love demands patience and kindness. It combines a refusal to resent with a commitment to the truth. It manages to treat people as people, to find space for them and to help them to flourish. These were formative days for me as I learnt how attentive and painstaking care for the quality of relationships in the staff-team and in the parish itself can turn hazardous situations into opportunities for deep friendship and great fun and so become transformative experiences of God's Spirit of love.

Some time later I found myself back in the world of theological education, charged with the responsibility of preparing men, and an increasing proportion of women, for ordained ministry. Again there has been a sense of history unfolding, not in the dramatic way of the vote and the first ordinations, which were by now a few years behind us, but in the slow awakening of the Church to the new situation that lay ahead. I say *awakening* because that is how it felt – and still feels.

Some of the awakening has been very personal. I think of a number of remarkably able Christian women for whom the ordination of any women, let alone themselves, had been unthinkable in all sorts of ways, some of them theological. And yet they had experienced God saying something different to them, calling them to discover their full stature in Christ. Watching them, helping them, encouraging them into life, seeing them extend and transcend themselves through theological study and ministerial practice has been a wonderful privilege.

Much of the awakening has been communal and institutional, affecting, for example, the way theological communities, like the ones in which I have been involved, live their lives and do their work. Our eyes are still being opened to the male culture systems of so much of what we do and the way we do it. We are still stretching out to reach the full gospel implications of the ordination of women for both training in and exercise of ministry. But it is good to see the light and feel the warmth of a new day upon us. The awakening from a long sleep has been going on, perhaps at an even slower rate, in the wider Church, as parishes and dioceses have begun to adjust their systems and expectations to a new set of possibilities for ministry. There is still a long way to go before the Church does more than merely cope with new eventualities but welcomes them as creative opportunities to develop an inclusive and holistic, collaborative and liberating ministry for a missionary age.

A few years ago I was asked to write a book on priestly ministry. At first I declined, thinking that the time had gone for a man from one tradition with one set of experiences to be writing a book about being a priest today. But I am grateful to Christine Smith of Canterbury Press for not letting the idea of the book go away, for I realized that I need not write all by myself. I could write it with someone else, a woman. I shared the idea with a colleague and she agreed to write it with me. The whole process of imagining the book, drafting it, discussing it and refining it *together* with Rosalind Brown was also a sort of awakening. I discovered that although we were able to contribute our different perspectives as people of different sexes, our fundamental under-standings, experiences and hopes for priestly ministry were very much the same. It was a renewed awakening to the Christ who loves and saves women and men and who calls us *together* into his life with God and with others.

*   *   *

Christopher Cocksworth is married to Charlotte and they have five children. They met and married at university, after which Christopher taught religious studies and economics before training for ordination at St John's College, Nottingham. He served a curacy in Epsom and then joined the ecumenical chaplaincy team at Royal Holloway, University of London. Since then he has been involved in theological education, first as director of the Southern Theological Education and Training Scheme (STETS) and currently as principal of Ridley Hall, Cambridge. A member of the Church of England Liturgical Commission, Christopher has written various books and articles on the theme of worship and has recently co-written with Rosalind Brown, *Being a Priest Today* (Canterbury Press, 2002).

Pilgrimage to Priesthood

ANGELA BERNERS-WILSON

I had been a member of MOW since its inception in 1978 at St Martin-in-the-Fields. It was therefore with very mixed emotions that I learnt, in January 1994, that I would be the first woman in England to be admitted to the priesthood when the Bishop of Bristol ordained the women deacons from his diocese into the priesthood on 12 March 1994. Of course all 32 of us were being ordained at the same service, and technically no one is actually ordained until the final Amen of the service is pronounced. So really there was no such thing as 'first'. The bishop and I both stuck rigidly to these words at each of the scores of interviews we gave, but that did not stop the media going to town about me as the 'first woman'. A very mixed blessing, but at least it gave me the opportunity to speak out about women's ordination in a positive light.

Due to all the media exposure I was to receive literally hundreds of letters and cards of congratulations from all over the world, many from complete strangers, and some from long distant relatives whom I had never met before. Ninety-nine per cent of these were extremely positive, just a few were very negative, one man saying he would pray for my soul as I would be damned forever by going through with the ordination. Another even wrote a 20-page letter from a holiday in Spain quoting all the scriptures that showed this move was against God's plan. Notwithstanding all of that, I and my sisters in Bristol diocese awaited 12 March with eager anticipation. We had a special week-long retreat in January conducted by the Revd Robin Clark, who had to come over from Berkeley in California, to prepare us for becoming women priests – obviously there was no one eligible for that role model in this country. She came to our ordination, and many of our first communion celebrations, and has remained in touch ever since. Thank you Robin for your wisdom, humour and sound advice.

The following is what I wrote on the morning of our ordination on 12 March 1994, and was first published in 'Momentum' – Bristol diocesan MOW's newsletter:

The sky is blue and cloudless despite the weather forecast; the birds are chirping joyfully in the trees, the grass is beaded with dewfall and a wood pigeon takes off from the tree opposite my window, cocking his head at me as if to say, 'Your turn now to take flight and soar.'

It really is TODAY – I can still barely believe it. Last night, unable to sleep despite the wine at dinner and a walk down the driveway (of Glenfall retreat house) in the dark where the trees were etched against the starlit, velvet night sky, cathedral arches of nature as I walked down the aisle of the drive. So at five to midnight I crept down to the chapel, lit the votive candle in front of the altar icon and sat, cross-legged in my dressing gown on the floor, looking out of the windows to the shimmering lights of Cheltenham and Gloucester in the distance.

On a night such as this a baby was born in a far-off land in a stable. Tonight is the eve of a day that will go down in the ecclesiastical history books.

We will be the first. What a weight of expectation and hope, of anger and fear and rejection, but it IS right, so right, God's right.

So now I can sit on my bed in the new morning: 'This is the day that the Lord has made; rejoice and be glad in it' on my lips, calm in the eye of the storm, knowing that I am in the prayers and hearts of literally hundreds of friends and acquaintances, colleagues and strangers, not just in Bristol or England or Britain but all over the world.

Other random memories from that day: As we were taken through the gates of the retreat house in the coach, en route for Bristol Cathedral, someone spotted that a ewe had just dropped two newborn lambs. 'What sex are they?' responded another of my sisters, 'They must be a male and a female!' was the reply. What a fitting icon for what was about to happen. Women would, at long last take their place alongside their male colleagues behind the altar. For our struggle has not, contrary to many newspapers, been about women's lib in the Church, but about celebrating the equality of opportunity for all God's children, regardless of gender.

So now, almost ten years on from the vote at General Synod in November 1992, where are we on this journey? Well, there is still a long way to go, it is not yet possible for a woman to become a bishop, and there are few women in high office within the church. One cathedral dean, one archdeacon, a handful of area deans. But there are many women who serve as parish priests in a huge diversity of settings from rural parishes (my former neighbour in our deanery was team rector of eight parishes) to inner-city parishes. What is more important than the job description is the fact that so many of us are now simply 'getting on with the job' and being accepted. If I speak for myself, I was – rather to people's surprise I learnt in retrospect – appointed to a united benefice of two very traditional parishes, one of which used the Book of Common Prayer for almost all its worship. I do not believe that anyone had even heard of MOW, and yet they have accepted me, and my husband, and taken us to their hearts. Out of all the criticisms that I have received in the last six and a half years since I have been here (some deserved, some not), none has been due to my sex. Yes, there are some chauvinists in both my congregations, but they work with me and accept that I am their rector. What is important is the service of pastoral care and leadership in worship that I provide, not my gender. And I am very fortunate to have both a male NSM, and a woman reader, both of whom more than pull their weight in the parish and in worship. I try to work collaboratively with others, and resist any pedestal-putting-on. And yes, there are times when the going is tough, the hours are too long, the comments from people who don't understand why churchyard rules have to be implemented are hurtful, the next fund-raising project for the church roof seems far too slow, etc., etc., but it is also a privilege to be a priest.

I never cease to give thanks that I can now fulfil my vocation, preside at the parish Eucharist Sunday by Sunday, and be a parish priest. To work with, and be there for people from all ages and different social backgrounds, from one day to 102 years, in their moments of joy and sorrow. To do baptisms, take weddings, and comfort the bereaved at the funeral of their life's partner is a tremendous joy and a privilege, for which I thank God.

*   *   *

Angela Berners-Wilson was born in 1954 and educated at the Convent of the Sacred Heart (RC) in Tunbridge Wells and Benenden School in Cranbrook. She then went to St Mary's College, University of St Andrews, Cranmer Hall, St John's College, University of Durham and WCC Graduate School, Ecumenical Institute at Bossey, Celigny, Geneva, Switzerland. Angela was ordained deaconess in St Paul's Cathedral in 1979, deacon in Southwark Cathedral in 1987, and priest in Bristol Cathedral on 12 March 1994. She was Senior Anglican Chaplain at the University of Bristol in 1991–95. Since then, Angela has been rector of the united benefice of St John the Baptist Church, Colerne, with St James the Great, North Wraxall. She is also on Diocesan Synod, the Diocesan Liturgical Committee, the Bishops Advisory Group for Healing, and the Vacancy in See Committee.

On Cathedrals and Committees

VIVIENNE FAULL

I stood at the back of Coventry Cathedral one Sunday morning
and a French women came up to me. 'You are a priest?' she
asked. 'Yes,' I replied, expecting to explain with pride how it is
that the Church of England has women who are ordained, and
then expecting an affirming smile or comment. But she continued, turning to one of my fellow canons, 'And is he a priest?'
'Yes'. 'And he also?' looking at the Dean and then at the
Succentor. 'You have four priests here?'

I have worked for the last decade in the enormously privileged
life of cathedrals; in Gloucester as chaplain, then as Canon
Pastor and Vice Provost of Coventry, and now as Provost, and
soon to be Dean, of Leicester. I have worked in teams of priests
who gave me confidence in my ministry as I learned from the
variety of theirs. Together we have worked in institutions which
still have a profound sense of purpose and significance.

Cathedrals are, mostly, very good places to be. So my priesthood has been formed by the experience of ministering to those
who have worshipped in cathedrals daily since early childhood,
as well as those who find cathedrals offer them anonymity as
they test out a new experience of faith in Jesus Christ. It has been
formed by the demands of ministering in the aftermath of the
discovery of the first bodies of young girls in Cromwell Street,
Gloucester; in the days after the death of Gill Phipps under the
wheels of a truck taking calves to a plane at Coventry airport; in
the days after the death of Diana. Above all, it has been formed
in the context of a corporate commitment to a cycle of daily
prayer and eucharistic thanksgiving, and the knowledge that our
business is God's business.

From my perspective in cathedrals, I have seen how communities have taken women priests to their hearts. There are now often
ordination services where the women candidates outnumber the

men. At the end of their deacon's year, the women return with stories that show how their gender is no longer an issue in their churches or, more particularly, in the wider community. And when I asked couples preparing for marriage if they are happy for me to take the service, they no longer understand why I am asking the question. Thanks to the sheer numbers of women priests (and, no doubt, the vicars of Dibley and Ambridge) we are no longer peculiar.

Yet there are times and places when my priesthood is not recognised by my church, and that sense of being a questionable priest impinges on my sense of vocation and my sense of identity. When I worked on the committee to prepare the legislation to enable women to be priested, I was told that we would have to allow parishes space to opt out of equal opportunities legislation and opt for male clergy. The committee was eventually persuaded that parliament would require 'compensation' for clergy who felt they had to resign over the priesting of women. The implication of these provisions was carefully argued.

In the weeks following the vote, new concerns emerged about collegiality in the House of Bishops, and about women who might be candidates for priesthood in diocese where the bishop could not, in conscience, ordain. The Act of Synod was passed with rather less thorough consideration than the enabling legislation. As a result, Leicester Cathedral sometimes arranges two services of priesting, one at which the diocesan bishop presides, another at which a bishop who does not ordain women presides. I also sometimes arrange two services for the annual renewal of ordination vows, one for the Bishop of Leicester, another for the Bishop of Richborough, our Provincial Episcopal Visitor. When the diocesan bishop presides I know I am a priest. When the Bishop of Richborough presides there are many present who are sure that I am not. And I begin to wonder, too.

When I cheered outside Church House Westminster in 1992 (and was hugged by complete strangers in Great Smith Street and congratulated by commuters on Paddington Station), what was being celebrated was, I believe, something much more that the possibility of a small group of women in England being able to become priests. At my theological college in the 1970s, the ethicist David Cook had put a stark question to us: 'Are women people too?' On 11 November 1992, the Church of England seemed to be saying, 'yes'. But a few months later, in passing the Act of Synod, its response seemed less assured. It said, at least as I heard it, 'well probably'.

So the theological debate (argued with energy in the 19th century, when women in the Church of England were first made deaconesses) continues over Biblical texts, and the authority of the Church of England, and what it means to be human, and the significance of Jesus' maleness. These are questions of the utmost importance, not just for our ministry, but for our mission.

In the city in which I live, being a women and a priest seems to provoke people to conversations about theology and about faith. Leicester is a city where faith matters. And being a woman of faith, holding office in the Church, seems to break down barriers between faith communities and between generations, rather than create them. But within the institutional life of the Church of England, women who are priests are seen as posing a problem as often as an opportunity. It will be some time yet, I believe, before the Church will be able to respond to that question, 'Are women people too?', with an unequivocal, and thrilling, 'absolutely'.

*　　*　　*

Viv Faull became a deaconess twenty years ago and worked at Mossley Hill Parish Church in Liverpool. Her training incumbent, Ken Riley, moved to Liverpool Cathedral soon afterwards and is now Dean of Manchester. When his other trainee from the 1980s became Bishop of Chester, Ken wrote to say 'Viv, if you can't become a Bishop like Peter, at least you can become a Dean like me!'. Ever respectful of her training incumbent, she moved from a chaplaincy at Clare College, Cambridge, to work at the cathedrals in Gloucester and later Coventry, becoming Provost of Leicester in 2000. Following her transformation into a Dean in 2002, the post of Provost has become extinct in the Church of England.

Women Bishops: Looking Forward

MARTYN PERCY

I suspect that I am not alone in surmising that one of the main reasons the vote to ordain women to the priesthood went through in 1992 was related to the issue of public credibility. Like many people who stood outside Church House on 11 November 1992, I went to a nearby pub to celebrate after the voting was announced. I have never quite got over the fact that hundreds of people in the pub – none of them, as far as one can tell, churchgoers – were genuinely pleased for the Church. There were pats on the back, cries of 'welcome to the twentieth century!', and even a few drinks bought. I cannot imagine what it would have been like trying to be part of the public face of the Church of England had the vote gone the other way.

No matter what theological arguments there are against women priests or women bishops (and there are very few that work well in Anglican theology), the Church of England is obliged to be a publicly credible body as much as it is mysterious. The argument for or against women bishops can never just be about convincing stalwart church members; *the arguments have to convince a nation*. One of the remarkable facets of the vote in 1992 was the realization that a large majority of the nation *wanted* the ministry of women priests; that they would take them to their heart as much as they warmed to the *Vicar of Dibley*. This is not meant to be a flippant remark. It is simply to underline that, culturally, the ground has shifted enormously over the last decade. Parishes that might have once been wary about a woman incumbent now grieve when they lose one. Team ministries invariably seek to strike a gender balance in the complementarity of their work. A women priest is an increasingly common sight in our nation – and one welcomed by many, if not most, people.

But what of women bishops? The heart of the dilemma for

those who are charged with coming to a common mind in the near future about women bishops is the identity of the Church of England, its theological methodologies and authorities. As members of the Rochester Commission will already know, the identity of the Church is disputed; the authorities that it uses to clarify its life and define its identity are invariably incomplete and contestable. There can be no appeal to an absolute authority to decide a theological question. Theological questions can only be settled by ongoing theological work, and by a process that tests itself through scripture, tradition and reason. The Church of England is the *via media*; thesis and antithesis wedded together in a tense but creative pastoral and theological synthesis.

My point about Anglican identity – and granted, much more could be said about this – reminds us that the Church of England does not own, and perhaps never has, the clear and settled ecclesiology that might be enjoyed by other denominations. Within the Church of England there has always been room for the tradition of 'loyal dissent', and this now extends, arguably, to the Anglican Communion as a whole. Thus, Anglicans in the diocese of Sydney can argue for (male) lay presidency at the Eucharist, and can trace their theological rationale not only in scripture, but also in tradition, by appealing to the seventeenth-century Puritan strain of Anglicanism that was once so influential. Thus, an apparently simple dispute about faith and order is not easily settled, since there is no one 'right' tradition that makes up Anglicanism. As a Church it is inherently plural; a pottage of competing convictions held together by liturgical, familial, doctrinal, cultural, theological and other ties. We need the complementarity of several distinctive traditions that on their own would be deficient.

Arguably, the question of women bishops is not one of those issues that can be settled definitively either way. The Anglican Communion is in a constant state of open process. That does not mean that it stands for nothing; nor does it mean that everything it tries and does is temporal or experimental. Rather, I choose the term 'open process' to remind us that Anglicanism has never been afraid of factoring praxis into its theological formulations and ecclesiological outcomes. It may be the case that women priests are, for some, within a period of reception. But the same is true for PEVs and the Act of Synod; proponents of women priests do not expect such things to endure either. The middle way – so beloved of Anglicanism – is to speak of integrities, and to try to get along in spite of difference (and perhaps because of it).

I rather doubt that women bishops in the Church of England pose quite the threat to unity that some suppose. There are already some Anglican provinces that have women bishops, and the Church of England is in full communion with those provinces. Although some English diocesan bishops would wish to conditionally reordain (male) priests who relocated from, say, the USA to England (presumably as deacons and then again as priests), there can be no escaping the fact that for the vast majority of Anglicans, globally and in England, the orders and ministry of such priests are already valid. It must be accepted that women priests are already a welcome development that most people in the Church and in the wider cultural sphere support. In time, women bishops will be demanded – as much from the nation the Church of England serves as from its own 'members'. It may be an astute and prudent form of public theology that anticipates this public (and spiritual) demand, and then goes on to show the Church in a more progressive light.

In a Church where compromise has often had to form the basis for communion, and where competing convictions have sometimes threatened to tear the Church apart, the debate offers a genuine opportunity to recover the *charity* that we Anglicans need to live together as faithful disciples, yet also as those who do not agree on certain matters of faith and order. A fuller appreciation of the richness and variety of traditions that make up the Anglican Communion – including those who espouse 'loyal dissent' – will help the Church come to a deeper understanding of its precious (if sometimes precarious) polity. But moving towards gaining women as bishops is, I believe, a necessary and important step for an established Church that wants and needs to be taken seriously as a public and inclusive body. May it happen soon.

*   *   *

Revd Canon Dr Martyn Percy is Director of the Lincoln Theological Institute, University of Sheffield. Previously he was Chaplin and Director of Studies at Christ's College, Cambridge. He is also a Council Member and Director of the Advertising Standards Authority, and a member of the Archbishops' Faith and Order Advisory Group. He has written a number of books, and is a regular broadcaster on Radio 4.

When I Saw Her Standing There

JOHN SAXBEE

Up until that moment, the idea of women priests was just that – an idea. Intellectually and theologically I had decided the matter to my personal satisfaction long ago, and was a fully paid up member of MOW. My manifesto for General Synod Elections said all the right things about how the time had come to put into practice what had already been agreed to in principle. No doubt I did all the right things to support women who felt they had a priestly vocation – though now I look back and cringe at my capacity to patronize them, as only those can who are in a role from which others are excluded. My right-on liberal credentials were impeccable, and I was much in demand to speak in support of women's ordination at all times and in all places. But the full weight and wonder of it all did not really dawn on me – until I saw her standing there.

The occasion was a run-of-the-mill voice training session on a regional ordination course. Course members were put through several exercises, including practice at standing at the altar eastward-facing, and speaking part of the eucharistic prayer. At that time, women could be made deacon but not ordained as priests. However, it seemed right for them to participate in this exercise, both to help their voice projection, and in anticipation of their priesting in due course. We used a large town church for this purpose, and after two or three of the men had been put through their paces, the first of the women took her turn. I went to the back of the church, and as I turned to look back up the aisle, I saw her standing there at the altar reading a passage of text. It was not her tone of voice or power of projection which struck me, so much as her posture which spoke to me of something new and different – not better or worse, but different. Suddenly an idea had taken on a semblance of reality, and I knew it must be only a matter of time before mere semblance became actuality.

This was in 1991, and a little over a year later I found myself emerging from Church House on 11 November, realizing that General Synod had done something which really made a mark in the world beyond those hallowed walls. People cheered or jeered us, but for once they did not ignore us. In cafés and bars, and back at the hotel it was a main topic of conversation initiated by those whose connection with the Church was at best a faint memory. It felt good to have been part of all of that – and that feel-good factor has marked mine and many other ministries ever since. It wasn't just that a long-cherished objective had been achieved, or that a justice denied by being so long delayed had now been honoured. It had something to do with being part of a Church which had claimed its wholeness as the people of God. To be whole is to be healed, and those of us who felt that we had been part of an infirm and unwholesome Church could now take up our bed and walk tall.

Not that the Church is no longer dis-eased. We have had to wrestle with the practicalities of co-existence with those whose hearts were broken by the very thing which made us feel whole. We have been careful to resist a couldn't-care-less triumphalism which applies salt rather than balm to open wounds. We have had to bear outrageous insults and discourtesies from those whose depth of opposition to women priests is not matched by any breadth of Christian charity. We have had to search in vain for signs of reciprocity on the part of those who avail themselves of resolutions to 'protect' themselves from women priests or liberal bishops, but who deny to parishes bound by their decisions the chance to seek pastoral oversight elsewhere.

Yet it has all been worth it, as we have experienced the ministry of women priests, and seen that ministry received and celebrated across our land. It has been so encouraging when, as an archdeacon conducting vacancy meetings, I have experienced parishes showing positive enthusiasm for women candidates to be considered for the posts. This has occasionally been in benefices where the previous incumbent had virulently opposed women priests, and tried to persuade his people likewise, but they refused to be cowed. Other times, the decision by parish representatives to nominate a woman as the preferred candidate has triggered many a case of cold feet, until the new priest arrives and all is well. But in most cases, issues of gender recede quickly into the background as people realize just how natural and right it feels to have men and women ministering together, as part of an inclusive priesthood.

Of course, a price has had to be paid by many women priests who have found themselves bearing the burden of anger and hurt projected on to them as if they should be scape-goated for what the Church as a whole had done. It has not been all about wholeness leading to happiness, and I think many of us have to ask ourselves just how much we have exacerbated problems for women priests by so wanting them to succeed, that we have pressurized them with expectations no male priests are expected to bear. Perhaps we will only be fully a whole and healthy Church when a woman priest can go ill, or astray, or slightly dotty without women's ministry as a whole being thereby diminished – as if male clergy didn't just occasionally fall victim to these all too human experiences!

We now look to the future and long for the time when gender no longer plays any part in determining who can minister where and when in the Church of God. For all the euphoria surrounding the ordination of women to the priesthood, we still have some way to go before that ministry is fully accepted. And of course there is the matter of women being considered for consecration as bishops. We will only be able to speak with assurance about a fully inclusive and non-gender-specific ministry when we can look to the episcopal president at a confirmation or ordination service – and see her standing there.

*   *   *

Born in Bristol in 1946, Bishop John is the youngest of five children. He was educated at Cotham Grammar School, and at Bristol and Durham universities where he read theology, and researched the writings of the Danish philosopher Søren Kierkegaard. He was ordained in Exeter Cathedral in 1972, and served as a curate, an incumbent and then as director of training in the diocese of Exeter. In 1992 he was appointed archdeacon of Ludlow, and two years later combined this post with that of suffragan bishop in the diocese of Hereford. In December 2001 he was appointed Bishop of Lincoln. He is a founder member of the College of Evangelists, president of the

Modern Church People's Union, vice-chairman of Springboard, and a long-standing member of General Synod. Throughout his ministry he has been actively involved in theological education and training, and is the author of *Liberal Evangelism* (SPCK 1994 – and still in print!). He has experience of ministry in urban, rural, market town and coastal communities, which characterize the diocese of Lincoln.

Facing the Light

LUCY WINKETT

It is the irresistible invitation, the unrefusable, compelling nature of being a priest that holds me and enthrals me. Being a priest for me is about turning my face towards the light, noticing that my internal compass needle keeps returning to the same direction in which I must travel.

I feel captured by priesthood. The way of life is sometimes exhausting, sometimes overwhelming and always demanding. But it is an abundant life. It is real.

I am not a mother, but I notice that some of the things I say resonate with my friends who are. Sometimes I am so wrapped up in the direction, pace and momentum of others' lives I can't remember my favourite colour or my preferred food; in short, I don't remember what I want or what I'm like. Being so involved with others has its advantages too; even when I have not known what I'm doing in a place or in a situation, the people around me have always known what I am doing there and they help me to define what I am called to be and do.

For me, being a priest is often about travelling at the speed of the other person; about learning to read the landscape around me and talking with others about what we can see.

I am in a small flat that smells faintly of incontinence pads which are in the bathroom. The two elderly ladies I am sharing a communion service with are laughing with me at the recent press coverage of my move to St Paul's. It is the last time I shall visit them before I move. We finish the service with the bread and wine balanced on the little table on wheels covered by a crocheted blanket. I pack up my home communion set; we hug and kiss and say goodbye. As I shut the door behind me I feel my eyes pricking and I sit on the stone stairs in the stinking stairwell and cry. It is not just the parting, but the grief at our communion; death and resurrection are acted out in the immobile lives of my congregation of two – reaching their hands forward for food and drink that God gives in abundance and I can bring to them. It is truly good news that I bring: companionship, gossip from the parish, silence and sacrament, and prayer for the dead loved ones that live so vibrant in their memory. Good news: I am also an evangelist.

An older priest tells me she will come to a difficult funeral with me, just to be there. I am touched and relieved that there will be someone to share this day with me. A traditional Nigerian funeral for a 29 year old woman and her baby means that the coffin lid is open as we lower her into the grave. I am not sure my legs will support me as I try to hold the grief of her family within the sacred words of the committal. They start to sing and I am reassured, calm and confident in the resurrection of Jesus and of his children lying dead before me.

I return immediately to the church to take a wedding. The same day: two families; one distraught, one overjoyed. I must be both.

The family celebrating the wedding do not need to know the scene I have just left and so I don't tell them. It is one of the hardest days of my ordained life, but I am being the person I love to be; the one who accompanies whatever the circumstances or facts of the life beside me.

My personality is one that relishes the unknown and my own particular life experience has brought to my soul the indelible marks of bereavement, intellectual endeavour and public exposure. I bring these experiences to my understanding of life as a priest, and my ministry is unavoidably shaped by them.

It is the character of Wisdom in the book of Proverbs who stands at the crossroads as she calls "to all that live". Standing at the crossroads, being at the margins of people's life experiences, is a place where I feel I can be the priest God calls me to be. Sometimes it is literally at society's margins; at 2 a.m., walking around the City of London with Social Services looking for people sleeping rough.

Sometimes I experience the margins at the heart of the establishment. The novelty of being a female priest is observed and remarked upon by the retired military men who organise the ceremonial life of the nation. There is a crossing of accepted boundaries that is part of my sacred task as a priest and I flourish there.

That the Church gives me authority to speak and to interpret the word of God publicly is a precious gift that I value and cherish. I find my sense of priesthood too in this public and symbolic role. As I sing the Eucharist or preach in the Cathedral, where I currently serve, I find my place in calling people beyond themselves; lifting them and holding them. I find my place in the process where human experience interacts with the ancient wisdom of Scripture, and we look for the signs of the presence of God in contemporary life.

I was at theological college on 11 November 1992. I had been selected for training to be a deacon, not a priest. Watching the television with other students, at the moment of frantic calculation to see whether the vote had been enough, I felt a man's hand on my shoulder as he said, 'Yes'. Much of what has happened in the past ten years has been fed by that 'Yes': God's 'Yes', which was never in doubt; my 'Yes', which so far has not left me; and the 'Yes' of the people of God for whom I am privileged and delighted to be a travelling companion and priest.

* * *

Lucy Winkett was born in 1968 in Wiltshire and grew up in Buckinghamshire. She spent a year in Australia teaching music before studying history at Selwyn College, Cambridge. She then worked variously as a history teacher, a professional singer, a barmaid and a photocopier demonstrator. During this time she lived in a L'Arche Community and trained at the Royal College of Music as a soprano. Her theological training was at Queen's College, Birmingham, and she served her title in Manor Park, East London. She was appointed a Minor Canon at St Paul's Cathedral in London in 1997, becoming the first ordained woman to be resident there.

Discovering the Kingdom

SUE HOPE

Some deep chord was touched in countless people that day – the day of the vote. I had the privilege of being there – being on the General Synod for that historic occasion. As I made my way back to Picadilly, to the hotel, I was overwhelmed with people: all sorts of people, black, white, female, male, rich, poor – the business man, the office cleaner, the shop assistant, the bus conductor, the woman with her shopping bags . . . I was overwhelmed with their joy! 'Well done!', 'Isn't it great?', 'Isn't it wonderful?', 'About time too!'

Something had been done. Something which resonated at a deep level. Something about God and women and there being a connection possible – and that was good news. Good news, not only for women, but for all, and especially for those who, up till then, had felt 'outside', on the margins. It seemed as though, for a while, people were hearing an echo of the kingdom, a kingdom whose music lay deeply hidden, submerged, forgotten in the psyche but whose memory was being reactivated powerfully through word and symbol. I felt that we were caught up in that kind of moment, and how exhilarating it was!

It's the kingdom that provokes my ongoing reflection on the priesthood. It is such joy to be a priest – to share in the celebration of community life, to weep with those who weep, to laugh with those who laugh, to minister the grace of the gospel, to stand back and feel awe as you see God doing his own work of transformation – and yet it has its shadow side. Oh, I don't mean the inevitable loneliness of leadership, the pains of ministry – not that kind of shadow. That's all part and parcel of the priesthood. By the 'shadow side' I'm thinking more of the truly dark – the issues around power, status and control. And I've seen those things, and the temptation to those things in me, and in others – both male and female. And that has set me thinking that we're only a very short way along the journey of the discovery of what the priesthood of the kingdom is about and that the step to ordain women is only the next step towards a much greater vision and a much more exhilarating end than we could possibly imagine. Because if now it's all complete, if now the questions about priesthood have all been answered – then why is the Church still so moribund, struggling, bound?

The shadow side can be clearly seen in our structures and our church life, but it can be seen chiefly in the silence of so many of the laity, in their lack of confidence, in their dependence upon a body of ordained people. It's perhaps most keenly felt in the eucharistic prayer itself – that great prayer of the Church – which belongs to the body yet remains, for the most part, firmly in the hands and on the lips of the individual priest him/herself.

If I've felt anger during my ministry as a priest it has been located around the issue of the clergy–lay divide. Surely this, what we have at the moment, isn't what priesthood is about? Surely there must be some greater picture, some deeper and better way of expressing the priesthood of all believers, of which we, as individually ordained people, are simply an icon?

For I am certain of one thing, and that is that the future of the Church belongs to the laity, and that somehow we, as priests, have got to find the way forward into a place as yet untravelled. Untravelled, but not unrecognizable. And when we get there, we'll recognize it as the place that we started from, because it's about the kingdom, and the music, though hidden from our ears, is still there, waiting to be discovered once more.

* * *

Sue Hope comes from a family of Anglican priests of many generations. She spent her childhood in Edinburgh and Hong Kong, and came to personal faith in the 1970s. She worked for St Michael-le-Belfrey, York, before training for ordination in Durham.

She served as a deaconess in West Yorkshire before moving to a second curacy in Sheffield diocese in the parish of Brightside and Wincobank. She was deacon-in-charge there, before being made vicar and then became vicar of St John's, Chapeltown.

She has just taken up a new post as Sheffield Diocesan Missioner. She has served on the General Synod and the Liturgical Commission and is a Six Preacher of Canterbury and an honorary canon of Sheffield Cathedral.

I Was Glad when They Said Unto Me, 'We Will Go Into the House of the Lord'

JO BAILEY WELLS

All I knew through my student days – long before I ever identified a call to ordination – was that I longed to work at something I *believed* in. I wanted to integrate my head and my heart, my work and my leisure, my professional life and my personal life. I contemplated counselling; I thought of social work; I considered teaching.

The ordained ministry has given me plenty of opportunity to explore all of these. As a college chaplain I much enjoyed being a Jill of all trades and mistress of none. No day ever lacked variety or spice – only space! I recall once beginning the day with a pastoral encounter exploring a suspected rape, moving swiftly to the champagne and roses of a graduation Eucharist, and later slipping out to the hospital on hearing of a student's attempted suicide. The blend of the sublime and the ridiculous, invariably flavoured with the tragic, drew me deeper into dependence on God. I found in his service all the excitement and joy one could wish for – in short, perfect freedom.

One moment during my last term as chaplain encapsulated that sheer joy. It was a wedding I conducted for two students I had come to know particularly well. Both had sung in the chapel choir, served as chapel wardens and participated in various study groups over a number of years. They represented the community I had sought to nurture. The familiar faces that gathered felt like the multitude that no one could number – and they could certainly sing with a loud voice! As the bride entered – beaming confidently – they sang out Parry's anthem, 'I was glad, *glad* when they said unto me . . .', lifting the roof off with their vigour and bringing tears to every eye, including those of the person who was leading the service. It was a scintillating coincidence of exuberance and beauty. I nearly fainted with the emotions of the occasion – I was indeed *glad* to have entered the house of the Lord.

As a college dean, I sought to make the workings of the college human and its worship divine. I was both priest and leader in a predominantly secular community where nothing about the priestly role could be taken for granted. I took on a host of public, institutional mantles, requiring discretion, patience, and diplomacy – yet I refused to let go of my more informal style, my desire to offer genuine friendship, my love of spontaneity and my need to express my own character at work as at home. Gradually I found the confidence to find a creative harmony between the given role and the possibilities it offered. I developed my own teaching style that broke with some of the didactic deductive norms. I encouraged the re-establishment of a college pottery where clay could *legitimately* be thrown at will. I moulded Prayer Book liturgy in order to interpret choral evensong for a twenty-first-century context. And above all, I maintained a genuine open-door policy with the promise of a listening ear to those of any faith or none on *any* subject, accompanied by coffee, chocolate, tissues or gin to suit the occasion. Continuing to unite the personal and the professional – so integral to my life and calling – was costly but so exciting. To command respect without a heavy handed show of authority; to be discreet yet available on two sides of a fence in a hierarchical world – these were the standards I strove for as I played with expectations and perceptions of being a young woman in an old man's job. Students and colleagues constantly nudged, provoked and challenged me to question and reassess my own assumptions and prejudices.

During my last year as dean there were several deaths within the college community, two of which were especially memorable and brought home forcefully how privileged is the strategic position of a priest. There was a fatal traffic accident while a student crossed the road. As I commended him to God ('Go on your way, O Christian soul . . .') at the end of the funeral, surrounded by a vast and anguished company of family and friends, I felt acutely the raw ends – the agonizing mess, the host of 'if onlys' – at a life cut short.

A week later I found myself planning another big funeral. A senior Fellow in his 90s, while on his way to a concert, had collapsed quite suddenly in the arms of his wife and his daughter. The previous day he had completed and posted the manuscript for his latest book. Here was a 'good' death. As I pronounced the exact same words of commendation, I felt the congregation release him with conviction and contentment. And the anthem the family had chosen – indeed, sang themselves! – as the coffin was brought in to the chapel was Parry's 'I was glad, *glad* when they said unto me . . .' I look back with much gladness myself, not only at that occasion, but on the circumstances and the community which sustained such opportunities for a priest – and indeed, a woman. It seems such a privilege to have found myself the first ordained female dean in such a situation.

A year ago I moved to Ridley Hall as Old Testament tutor. I still have the opportunity to accompany students (though very different ones), and I have even more opportunities to nurture vocations. But now I have more time to teach and less administrative responsibility. The position is rather more conducive for family life, a detail that has become significant since the recent birth of a child.

I once heard a female priest describe motherhood as the most formative experience of her ministry. I delight in the possibility of a working life that can be integrated with family life; indeed, it is another development of the original longing and call. Furthermore, colleagues have encouraged me concerning the relevance and importance of the balancing act for the very work of training future priests. This I see as the principle of the clergy stipend. The stipend is not so much remuneration for particular services rendered. It is the permission, trust and opportunity for a priest not to spend every moment covering over the cracks in their own mission, character and bank balance, but on the contrary to offer those cracks as a gift to God, and let the light of Christ shine through them, in a spectrum of wondrous ways.

I am indeed glad to have heard the invitation – and been granted the opportunity – to have entered the house of the Lord as one of God's priests.

*   *   *

Dr Jo Bailey Wells is a tutor at Ridley Hall, training men and women for ministry, and lecturer in Old Testament and Biblical Theology within the Cambridge Theological Federation. She was previously dean and chaplain of Clare College in Cambridge. Both before and after ordination she has relished opportunities for nurturing faith and vocation among students in Britain and overseas. She owes much to Christians in Uganda, Transkei and Haiti for the rekindling of her own faith. She is married to Sam, who is also a priest. Their son, Laurence, and their dog, Connie, are chiefly responsible for shaping their modest adventures, which regularly include a Norfolk beach and not-often-enough involve the French Alps.

Behold, I Am Doing a New Thing

PENNY JAMIESON

Whenever I return to England I reflect on where I might have been in my bid to serve God if I had not set sail with my new husband for New Zealand in the early months of 1965. And I am humbled.

Many of the women who were among those ordained priest in 1994 were the same age as I was and one had attended the same school as me. Yet I was in England as the invited guest of the MOW (the Movement for the Ordination of Women) to preside at its closing conference.

It is undoubtedly true that had I not moved to New Zealand all those years ago my own vocation to the ordained ministry would not have been as well-established as it was in 1994 when I was a four-year-old Bishop of Dunedin. My own journey had not been without its struggles and its setbacks, but these paled into insignificance compared with the lengthy struggle that my friends in the Church of England had endured. Over many years I have done my share of street-fighting for the cause of women's ordination, both in New Zealand and other countries.

Yet as I reflect on this I realize that there are many differences between the calling of a priest and the calling of a bishop. The mustard seed within that is the beginning of the calling of a priest is often quite a lonely experience. It has all the characteristics of a direct implant from God. It begins so small, but grows until it must break out of the heart that has sheltered it, and spread branches wide to make shelter for many others.

As a bishop, I have often offered shelter for women and men for whom the ache of vocation has become unendurable and demands to be heard. As a friend, I have offered shelter to women in other countries whose jurisdiction has been slow to recognize that God does indeed plant the seeds of calling to the priesthood in the hearts of women. And I have wept with them.

But, as I remember it some 12 years on, the call to be a bishop came not from my own heart but from the Church, and it was urgent, unexpected and overwhelming. After recovering from the initial sense of shock, I began the very necessary journey inward to listen for that still, small voice of God. For the longer I live in the ordained and ordaining ministry I realize what a cruel thing it is to ordain someone who is not called by God.

These differences in calling reflect some of the very practical differences in ministry between priests and bishops. In general, there are few limits on the numbers of priests that can be ordained. In the days when all priests were stipendiary, perhaps the numbers were limited by the numbers of the positions available, but although people were, and still are, ordained to a title, there was no direct relation between the call to ordination and the call to a particular ministry. The situation has loosened still further with non-stipendiary ordinations, so that there is now little restraint on the number of people who can be ordained to the priesthood.

By contrast, the call to the episcopate comes clearly labelled. It is a call to a particular and named episcopal position. And the number of these is, give or take any changes in policy effecting the appointment of assistant bishops, or the establishment or dis-establishment of a diocese, fairly constant in any one province. It therefore follows that the number of dioceses and other episcopal positions will, in effect, limit the number of ordinations to the episcopate. This leads inevitably, whether bishops are elected or appointed, to a sense of competition for each post and hence of competition for ordination.

Thus the context, if not the theology, of the debate about the ordination of women to the episcopate is very different from that of the ordination of women to the priesthood. It effectively means that if a woman becomes a bishop then a man will not, whether or not it is obvious who that man is. There is often in this situation a sense that a wrong has been done, and that someone who deserved the elevation has been cheated of it. It will take a long time for the expectations of clergy on this to change. I have often wondered whether it is this element of scarcity, of competitiveness that makes people want to become bishops. There is considerable power in possessing any commodity that is in short supply.

So why do people want to become bishops?

The most common and the most cynical response is that people become bishops for power. But I am not at all sure that this is the case. I think the call of God working within the Christian community has much more to do with it than we are ready to allow. We focus strongly on the task of discernment when we are working to identify those whom God has called to be priests. And without exception, all those whom I have ordained, both men and women, have claimed the call of God on their lives, and I have believed in that call myself. The signs of call were certainly what I was looking for when the diocese of Dunedin elected me to be their bishop. I think most bishops are compelled by their sense of their obedience to the call of God in the Church and are not silly enough to see power itself as a reason for becoming a bishop.

Bishops are, however, still surrounded by enormous images of power. We are familiar enough with the traditional ones. They are all marked by opulence, but in both Australia and New Zealand in recent years they have been reinforced very publicly by the elevation of an archbishop to be Governor General. Unquestionably bishops are both seen to have power and do have power. This is inevitable, and not in itself a bad thing, but the danger that I see lies not in the nature of power itself but rather in its seemingly inevitable tendency to become self-serving. This is the personal and spiritual challenge of every bishop and indeed of all clergy. Too often the privileges of our position lead to the development of a spirit of entitlement which not only is damaging to the soul but also undermines the message of divine love which is at the heart of the gospel. I have no reason to believe that women are immune to this distortion of vocation.

Perhaps the problem is more with the role that bishops play. I believe that the Church as a whole places far too much importance on the position of bishops. In fact I think they are a relic of a bygone age and of a bygone God whose major concern was to order and discipline his subjects. If we had more trust in the wisdom of God's self-revealing love from within the corporate life of the Christian community, the body of Christ, we would probably preoccupy ourselves more with the concerns of Jesus than with the structures of order and power and control that soak up such a huge amount of unproductive energy within the

Church. The 1998 Lambeth Conference illustrated this all too well.

So as the Church of England moves forward in this debate it is really important to keep eyes squarely on the gospel imperative to live the love of Christ and make it real in our world. It is all to easy to traduce righteous cause, the just war, into the opposite of what it stands for. It is all too easy to make the cause of women the cause of the campaign and that, in turn, would deflect attention from the call on all followers of Jesus Christ to live the love of God authentically in the mission of the good news of Christ. A collective commitment to reimaging the role of bishops in offering a leadership of love and grace for all is central to the project.

The call for this to happen is coming from many places these days, but always from people who are living on the edge, or beyond the edge, of the institutional Church. It has become unfortunately obvious that institutional structures all too easily betray God by their protection of God. What I say echoes the strong call of many for a fresh engagement with Jesus and fresh insight into the creative liberty of God. Because that liberty is freely shown and freely given, we see it as inseparable from care, love, grace. It is never control and power. Creativity is gift and nurture; it is call, it is invitation, and it is essentially self-diffusing and self-sharing. It is a leadership of love that permeates the entire community and to share in it means that we are called to share it with others. So our participation in God's liberty is necessarily a participation in the act of making free. This is a call to the leadership of the Church, whether lay or ordained, whether male or female. We have come a long way in reimagining the role of clergy; it surely is time to turn the spotlight on both the laity and the episcopate.

Perhaps the opportunities afforded by the current debate in England on the ordination of women as bishops will afford opportunity for these issues to be considered further.

*   *   *

Penny Jamieson was born in England and has lived most of her adult life in New Zealand. She has a grown family and has worked with Pacific Island peoples in the area of first language maintenance. Ordained for 20 years and Bishop of Dunedin for

12 years, Penny has lead the Diocese through challenging changes, including the development of theological education and the changing role of the church in public life. She has spoken and written extensively on the subject of church leadership. Her book *Living on the Edge: Sacrament and Solidarity in Leadership* was published in 1997 (Mowbray).

Postscript

CHRISTINA REES

The voices we have heard in this book are part of a much larger group of ordained women and men in the Church of England who believe passionately that God calls people for many reasons and to many ministries, but not on the basis of their sex. In this, God is without sexual prejudice and is gender-blind, both in how God considers human beings and in the nature of the Godself. In the Gospels we see Jesus relating to a wide variety of people, drawing both women and men into his close circle of friends and disciples. We accept that his teaching and example were for all people. With the awareness of continuing injustice, discrimination and prejudice, we believe that Jesus came to show humanity a better way. We also believe that Jesus' death and resurrection and the coming of the Holy Spirit have equal significance and value for men and women alike.

The story of women's journey towards full inclusion and acceptance in the Church of England is a story that is still unfolding. We are working now for women bishops and for the laying to rest of the Act of Synod. We are questioning the Church's present exemption from the Sex Discrimination Act of 1975. We are asking the Church to be more honest and open in how it appoints and deploys people. We hold the vision of the Church as a community of equals.

In all this, we acknowledge and repent of our own unjust ways. We know ourselves, as individuals and as part of the institution of the Church, to need healing, forgiveness and mercy. We recognize sins of omission as well as sins of commission, and we are all too aware of our fear and lack of courage.

It is because of our faith in a loving and merciful God, who delights in us and who is always reaching out to us – in 'blessedness and joy' as Mother Julian puts it – that we know ourselves to be loved and called to be part of the body of Christ. We are confident that we are members of Christ's body and rejoice in the gift of God's Holy Spirit, trusting that 'by one Spirit we were all baptized into one body' (1 Corinthians 12:13).

We believe that Paul's passionate plea to the Christians at Ephesus speaks of a unity that can be ours, when he writes:

I, therefore, the prisoner for the Lord, beg you to lead a life worthy of the calling to which you have been called, with all humility and gentleness, with patience, bearing with one another in love, making every effort to maintain the unity of the Spirit in the bond of peace. There is one body and one Spirit, just as you were called to the one hope of your calling, one Lord, one faith, one baptism, one God and Father of all, who is above all and through all and in all. (Ephesians 4:4–6)

We believe that God is the One who calls, to faith and obedience and also to specific ministries, both ordained and lay. It is for God to decide and for the Church to respond. As members together of Christ's body, we need each other if we are to promote 'the body's growth in building itself up in love' (Ephesians 4:16).

When Jesus prayed his great prayer to his Father, speaking of a unity beyond human making, he was holding in his heart and mind *all* people. The unity of the Trinity invites all to join in the Dance: 'so the love with which you have loved me may be in them, and I in them' (John 17:26).

When women and men can join in the Dance as equals, able both to lead and to follow, to hold and to release, then the world will see, and will be drawn also into the Dance, and much, much more of the kingdom of God will have come on earth.

Epilogue

ROWAN WILLIAMS

The two thoughts that occur to me, reflecting on this remarkable and moving material, are both to do with how we think about the Church itself. If we are serious in thinking that the Church exists as something more than just a human association of like-minded people, but is a gift created by God's act, then change and development in the Church must be more than the accrual of fresh, good ideas. You don't have to agree in all respects with Newman on the development of doctrine to see that the moments of significant newness in the Church's history, language and practice need to be understood as an uncovering of connections and resonances in our central doctrines that have never before been 'brought out in performance', as we might say. The analogy is serious: a good, new Shakespearean production may shake us up in its unconventionality, but if it is really good it will make us say, 'I never saw that,' so that we go away from the theatre not thinking about a new and different play, but ready to read and ponder in a way that shows new depths in what we thought was familiar.

The most substantial argument for the ordination of women, I have always believed, is the simple one that connects with baptism. If women cannot be ordained, then baptised women relate differently to Jesus from baptised men – not a doctrine easily reconcilable with the New Testament. But if so, then we ought to be discovering in the light of women's ordination some new depths in our understanding of baptism, especially of what it is to be baptised into the 'priestliness' of Jesus. We ought to be recovering the sense of the centrality in discipleship of what William Stringfellow, the great American lay theologian, called 'advocacy' – speaking to God and to God's world on behalf of those isolated from God by suffering or humiliation, self-hatred and sin. We ought to be recovering a sense of what the Church's distinctive voice is – Jesus' voice, speaking to God in intimacy, speaking to the world in challenge and hope. What the Church says at the Eucharist is the expression of this baptised identity, simultaneously turned towards Jesus' 'Abba' and to all those hungry and thirsty for God and God's justice.

New acquisitions to a sacred caste are neither here nor there; that would be a development at best indifferent to, and at worst destructive of, the integrity of doctrine. What we should be looking for and praying for is the revived commitment to what the identity in Christ of the baptised is all about; only then can the ordained effectively do their distinctive job of telling and showing the Church what it is.

And so, very briefly, to the second thought. We hear a good deal about 'reception'; but it's often talked about as if it were a consultation process (document embargoed until 21 June; responses to the Welsh Office by 22 June at the latest . . .). What's the deadline? What are the criteria? How strong a consensus? But in the light of what I've just said, the real 'reception' would be in the condition of a Church visibly more conscious of its baptismal charism. We'd look less for a satisfactory headcount, more for a practical and theological shift of priorities. Much harder to measure, of course, but more obviously connected with why the whole thing mattered in the first place. And if even theoretical opponents of women's ordination have been forced to much deeper reflection on the nature of the baptismal grace by this debate – as I think has indeed happened – that too is part of the real process of reception – the fresh performance of our 'text', so that we see more, not less, in the tradition we share.

So I hope that the next phase of our church life will show some intense reflection on this and its implications, as we thank God for the witness borne by ordained women to the one thing that matters: the gift of being in Christ, speaking with Christ, acting for Christ, as a community representing the new creation.

Archbishop Rowan

Printed by BoD™in Norderstedt, Germany